MATHEMATICAL
APPLICATIONS

Deane Arganbright
MATHEMATICAL APPLICATIONS OF ELECTRONIC SPREADSHEETS

McGraw-Hill Book Company

New York   St. Louis   San Francisco   Auckland   Bogotá
Hamburg   Johannesburg   London   Madrid   Mexico
Montreal   New Delhi   Panama   Paris   São Paulo
Singapore   Sydney   Tokyo   Toronto

To Susan, Nate, and Andy

Library of Congress Cataloging in Publication Data

Arganbright, Deane.
  Mathematical applications of electronic spreadsheets

  Bibliography: p.
  Includes index.
  1. Mathematics—Data processing. 2. Electronic spreadsheets. I. Title.
QA76.95.A7 1984   510′.285′4   84-7117
ISBN 0-07-002429-4

1 2 3 4 5 6 7 8 9 0   DOC/DOC   8 9 8 7 6 5 4

ISBN 0-07-002429-4

The editors for this book were Stephen G. Guty and Philip E.
McCaffrey, the designer was Elliot Epstein, and the production
supervisor was Teresa F. Leaden. It was set in Century
Schoolbook by Bi-Comp, Incorporated.

Printed and bound by R. R. Donnelley & Sons Company.

CalcStar is a trademark of Micropro International Corp.,
Multiplan is a trademark of Microsoft Corporation, 1-2-3 is a
registered trademark of Lotus Development Corporation,
PerfectCalc is a trademark of Perfect Software, Inc., SuperCalc
is a registered trademark of Sorcim Corporation, and VisiCalc
is a registered trademark of VisiCorp, Inc.

Contents

Demonstrations of Circular Reference   139

Preface

The electronic spreadsheet, of which VisiCalc was the first developed and best known version, is one of the most popular microcomputer software products. Designed for financial modeling and forecasting, it is powerful and versatile yet easy to use. Financial models are implemented using a spreadsheet program by entering both numerical data and algebraic expressions and organizing the data into a large matrix, or spreadsheet. The spreadsheet program calculates values for each of the expressions and displays the data and the calculated values in a spreadsheet format on the computer screen. By changing entries in the matrix a user can modify the hypotheses or parameters of the model. When an entry is changed, the value of each expression in the entire spreadsheet is recalculated and the screen display immediately updated. This allows a user to obtain answers quickly to a variety of "What if . . . ?" questions. With its visual format and interactive updating features, the electronic spreadsheet has proved to be a valuable tool for economic modeling, business forecasting, scheduling, projecting, and numerous similar applications.

The electronic spreadsheet can also be used effectively and creatively in mathematics. Algorithms that are recursive, iterative, or adaptable to a table format can often be implemented easily and naturally on a spreadsheet, allowing the user to change initial values, step sizes, and other parameters and see the result of the changes instantly. Moreover, many applied mathematics problems can also be set up, analyzed, and solved on a spreadsheet. The what-if features of the spreadsheet make it useful in mathematical modeling, the design and study of algorithms, problem solving, and the study of mathematics.

This book demonstrates spreadsheet implementations of algorithms from extensive areas of mathematics. It is written for a wide audience, including those who are interested in exploring mathematical ideas and those who enjoy finding new applications for electronic spreadsheets. The examples illustrate a wide variety of mathematical concepts and techniques. Many of them require only advanced high school mathematics; others make use of concepts found throughout the college mathematics curriculum. Some demonstrations are designed specifically to require user interaction in intermediate steps, and all have interactive aspects.

The book can be used as the basis for the personal study of a variety of interesting mathematical topics. Creating a mathematical spreadsheet model provides an excellent stimulus for mathematical growth. In developing a spreadsheet implementation for an algorithm or in preparing a classroom demonstration using a spreadsheet, I have found that other algorithms, topics, or ideas to pursue invariably arise. Study of these subjects then uncovers additional results, alternative derivations, and previously unexamined ideas. In short, the use of the electronic spreadsheet in mathematics encourages the *doing* of mathematics.

This book can also be used by teachers as a source of demonstrations to enhance the classroom presentation of mathematical topics, as a resource book for independent student projects, and as a supplementary text for courses in mathematics or computing. The demonstrations should also be useful in developing student assignments. The electronic spreadsheet can be used for these assignments in at least three modes:

1. Predesigned templates. A basic spreadsheet illustrating an algorithm or concept is created in advance and stored on a disk. Students load the disk, change the data and parameters, and observe the results.

2. Parallel adaptations. Students design spreadsheets that parallel pencil-and-paper algorithms or solution methods. Creating a spreadsheet becomes a productive activity in its own right, reinforcing the concept being studied. Many of the demonstrations in this book provide models for this approach.

3. Original creations. Students develop their own techniques for creating spreadsheets to model problems and implement algorithms. The examples presented here will give an idea of the many creative possibilities that exist.

Finally, there are a number of reasons why the electronic spreadsheet is an especially good means of integrating the computer into the study of mathematics:

- Spreadsheet operation is natural and easy to learn. Since it assumes no prior computer knowledge, a person with a modest mathematics background can be creating spreadsheets for algorithms and applied problems after a few hours of study and practice on a computer.

- Spreadsheets for algorithms follow the same format and techniques commonly used in doing the work by hand. Therefore creating a spreadsheet directly reinforces the concepts involved in the mathematical algorithm or problem being implemented.

- The spreadsheet format makes algorithms and manipulations concrete and easy to visualize. This not only makes algorithms easier to understand but also allows the user to concentrate more on an algorithm's structure and less on programming details.

- The what-if capabilities of a spreadsheet program allow a user to modify parameters easily and see the effects of the changes instantly.

- Learning how to use a spreadsheet program provides experience and skills that are valued in the business community.

Of course, there is another fundamental reason for doing mathematics on a spreadsheet: It's fun! Moreover, the range of possible applications seems unending. Many examples are presented in the book, and others are listed in the exercises. The reader is encouraged to find the challenge and enjoyment that come in discovering further uses of this exciting and creative tool.

I wish to express appreciation to my wife Susan, for her untiring support and for assisting with the illustrations; to Ray Hamel, for suggesting Demonstration 36; to Rod Hansen and Richard Schori, for their encouragement and advice; to Robert McCroskey and Whitworth College, for providing computer facilities; and especially to Howard Gage, for introducing me to the electronic spreadsheet, for his stimulating ideas, and for his valued friendship. Some of the concepts presented in this book have appeared in the March 1984 issue of *The College Mathematics Journal* and the *1984 Yearbook of the National Council of Teachers of Mathematics*.

Deane Arganbright

About the Author

Deane E. Arganbright is Professor and Chair of the Department of Mathematics/Computer Science at Whitworth College, Spokane, Washington. This book is the outgrowth of his work on developing new ways of using the computer in math studies. He is a frequent speaker at mathematics and computer science conferences and a contributor to the math journals, including *The College Mathematics Journal, The Mathematics Teacher,* and the *Pacific Journal of Mathematics.*

Basic Spreadsheet Operation

This chapter surveys the basic ideas of spreadsheet operation and provides sufficient background for the implementations of the mathematical algorithms and examples in this book. More complete discussions of the features, commands, and other operational aspects of a spreadsheet program can be found in user's manuals and books, many of which are listed in section B of the References at the end of the book.

Since the initial development of VisiCalc, many other spreadsheet programs have appeared, e.g., SuperCalc, PerfectCalc, CalcStar, Multiplan, and 1-2-3. Each has its own notation and methods for implementing the basic operations. Although the discussion in this chapter is based on VisiCalc, it is generally descriptive of other spreadsheet programs. User's manuals should be consulted for specific details and comparisons.

Throughout this book *electronic spreadsheet* or *spreadsheet program* refers to the program itself, e.g., VisiCalc or SuperCalc, while *spreadsheet* is used to describe both the display format and the set of all expressions and cell locations for a given implementation. References are indicated by numbers in brackets, e.g., [12].

I-1 A FINANCIAL SPREADSHEET EXAMPLE

Business models and financial analyses are often contructed in the form of rectangular tables, or matrices, called *spreadsheets*. Spreadsheets are employed extensively in accounting for balance sheets, ledgers, depreciation schedules, inventory records, financial projections, and cash-flow analyses. In a spreadsheet presentation both data and the results of computations are displayed in rows and columns.

Spreadsheets can be updated frequently as new information is obtained or hypotheses change. The following example illustrates a traditional spreadsheet application.

Example: A small college has developed a simple model to project its future budgets. To help administrators study the implications of the model, a member of the college staff has constructed a college budget spreadsheet (Figure I-1). The first column of the spreadsheet contains information from the current year's balanced budget. Subsequent columns are based on the following assumptions provided by the administrators:

- Enrollment will decrease by 3% annually.
- Tuition and salaries will both increase by 5% annually.
- Gift income will increase by 10% annually.
- Other costs are expected to rise by 8% annually.

It is clear from the spreadsheet that the college will incur large deficits if the assumptions hold true. Realizing this, the college administrators want to investigate the effects of modifying their assumptions by asking a number of what-if questions: What if enrollment can be maintained at 2000 each year? What if gift income can be increased by 20% each year? What if salaries are frozen during 1984–85? The answers to these questions will provide the administration with a basis for adopting policies that will lead to balanced budgets.

To see the effects produced by various combinations of modifications of the assumptions it is necessary to recalculate much of the spreadsheet over and over. Performed manually, this task is extremely time-consuming, even with models of a modest size. To implement such models easily and naturally on microcomputers Bricklin and Frankston developed the electronic spreadsheet program VisiCalc in the late 1970s [25]. Many similar programs have since been developed by others. An electronic spreadsheet model of the college budget example is presented in Section I-2, after a few fundamental electronic spreadsheet concepts have been described.

```
                        83-84   84-85   85-86   86-87

ENROLLMENT               2000    1940    1882    1825
TUITION                  5000    5250    5512    5788

INCOME (in thousands)
   Tuition              10000   10185   10374   10563
   Gift                  2000    2200    2420    2662
TOTAL INCOME            12000   12385   12794   13225

EXPENSES (in thousands)
   Salary                5000    5250    5512    5788
   Other                 7000    7560    8165    8818
TOTAL EXPENSES          12000   12810   13677   14606

NET                         0    -425    -883   -1381
```

Figure I-1 College budget.

I-2 FUNDAMENTAL SPREADSHEET CONCEPTS

A spreadsheet program uses a large matrix, or spreadsheet. The rows are identified by positive integers and the columns by letters (Figure I-2). Locations, or *cells,* in the matrix are identified by column and row, for example, D3. Each cell can contain a descriptive label, a number, or an algebraic expression which uses the values of other cells in the spreadsheet. Numbers and algebraic expressions are referred to as *values.*

The computer screen acts as a window into the spreadsheet, showing the labels, the numbers, and the values of the algebraic expressions stored in the cells of a portion of the spreadsheet. Most spreadsheet programs display 20 rows of the matrix. The number of columns shown is determined by the column widths set by the user. Special commands allow a user to display different sections and different amounts of the spreadsheet on the screen. A cursor, which can be moved to any cell, highlights one of the locations in the spreadsheet. The expression stored in the cell on which the cursor is placed can be changed by the user. Information about that expression is shown in the entry line at the top of the screen.

The cursor in the screen in Figure I-3 is located at cell B3. The entry line shows that the expression stored in cell B3 is .2*B2 and that it is a value (V). The C on the entry line indicates that recalculations of the spreadsheet will be carried out column by column. A user can also choose to have the spreadsheet recalculated row by row.

Figure I-4 provides a step-by-step illustration of the basic operation of a spreadsheet. The entry line has been condensed so that it contains only the cell coordinates and the expression entered into the cell. Calculations are performed row by row.

Comments on Figure I-4

1. A user can enter descriptive labels into the cells of the spreadsheet. (With the cursor at cell A1, enter the label SAMPLE.)

Figure I-2 Spreadsheet matrix.

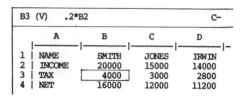

```
B3  (V)     .2*B2                              C-
|--------|--------|--------|--------|-
      A        B        C        D
1 |  NAME     SMITH    JONES    IRWIN
2 |  INCOME   20000    15000    14000
3 |  TAX       4000     3000     2800
4 |  NET      16000    12000    11200
```

Figure I-3   Spreadsheet screen.

2. Numbers can be stored similarly. (With the cursor at cell A2, enter the number 9.)

3. Algebraic expressions involving variables can be entered into cells. Variables obtain their values from the cells they refer to. The value of the expression in a cell is calculated by the program and appears on the screen. (With the cursor at cell B2, enter the expression 4*A2. Since the current value of A2 is 9, 36 appears on the screen in location B2. The expression 4*A2 is stored in cell B2.)

4. A spreadsheet program has a number of library (built-in) functions, including the square-root function. [With the cursor at cell A3, en-

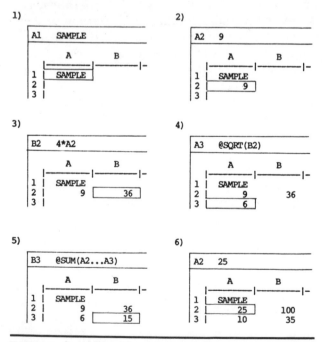

Figure I-4   Spreadsheet operation.

ter @SQRT(B2). The square root of the current value of B2 is 6, and it appears in cell A3].

5. Certain functions of several variables are also available, including the SUM function. [Place the cursor at B3 and enter @SUM(A2...A3) to find the sum of the entries in column A from cell A2 to cell A3. The sum, 15, appears in cell B3 on the screen.]

6. Finally, if an entry in a cell of the spreadsheet is changed, all entries in the spreadsheet that refer to it in any way are updated. (Place the cursor on cell A2 and enter 25. Not only is the value of cell A2 changed but also that of cells A3, B2, and B3.)

In describing the formulas stored in the spreadsheet it is convenient to present them in the table format of Figure I-5, which describes the example of Figure I-4 at step 6. The examples in this book will follow this format.

It is now possible to describe a spreadsheet implementation for the college budget in Section I-1. One such implementation is given in Figure I-6, where all dollar amounts are shown in thousands. The growth rates given by the original assumptions of the model have been entered into column A as parameters. Formulas for calculations based on these parameters appear in columns C, D, and E. For example, the formula in cell D4 for the 1984–85 tuition, (1+A4)*C4, is the product of the tuition growth factor (1+A4) and the tuition for 1983–84 (C4). This spreadsheet will generate the college budget spreadsheet displayed in Figure I-1. As the values of the parameters are changed, the spreadsheet is recalculated, showing the result of the modifications instantly. In particular, if the value of cell A8 is set to .2 (giving a 20% growth rate in gift income), then the net figure for 1985–86 (cell E16) becomes −423 rather than the −883 obtained from the original assumptions.

In working with a spreadsheet, a few conventions must be observed closely:

1. When a cell entry is changed, each expression in the entire spreadsheet is recalculated automatically. (A "manual" recalculation option permits the user to defer recalculation until a specific command has been entered.) This updating is done row by row or column by

```
          A                 B
   |----------------|----------------|-
1  | SAMPLE
2  | 25               4*A2
3  | @SQRT(B2)        @SUM(A2...A3)
```

Figure I-5 Spreadsheet formulas.

column, as selected by the user. The order in which the calculations are performed must be taken into account in designing spreadsheets.

2. In some spreadsheet programs algebraic operations are carried out using the usual operator precedence relations. In others, e.g., VisiCalc, operations in formulas and expressions without parentheses are performed left to right in the order in which they appear. In this case, 6*2+3*4 is 60, not 24. Expressions in this book are displayed in an unambiguous form, for example, (6*2)+(3*4).

3. In some spreadsheet programs (including VisiCalc) any expression beginning with a letter is treated as a label. Therefore a formula that begins with a cell location must include an initial operation sign, +A4*B6, or parentheses, (A4*B6). This convention is adopted

Formulas

	A	B	C	D	E
1			83-84	84-85	85-86
2	INCR %				
3	-.03	ENROLL	2000	(1+A3)*C3	(1+A3)*D3
4	.05	TUITION	5	(1+A4)*C4	(1+A4)*D4
5					
6		INCOME			
7		TUIT	+C3*C4	+D3*D4	+E3*E4
8	.10	GIFT	2000	(1+A8)*C8	(1+A8)*D8
9		TOTAL	+C7+C8	+D7+D8	+E7+E8
10					
11		EXPENSE			
12	.05	SALARY	5000	(1+A12)*C12	(1+A12)*D12
13	.08	OTHER	7000	(1+A13)*C13	(1+A13)*D13
14		TOTAL	+C12+C13	+D12+D13	+E12+E13
15					
16		NET	+C9-C14	+D9-D14	+E9-E14

Screen Output

	A	B	C	D	E
1			83-84	84-85	85-86
2	INCR %				
3	-.03	ENROLL	2000	1940	1881.8
4	.05	TUITION	5	5.25	5.5125
5					
6		INCOME			
7		TUIT	10000	10185	10373.
8	.1	GIFT	2000	2200	2420
9		TOTAL	12000	12385	12793.
10					
11		EXPENSE			
12	.05	SALARY	5000	5250	5512.5
13	.08	OTHER	7000	7560	8164.8
14		TOTAL	12000	12810	13677.
15					
16		NET	0	-425	-883.9

Figure I-6 College budget model.

in this book, and any expression beginning with a letter is treated as a label. Labels not beginning with a letter can be entered by first typing a quote (") symbol. Some spreadsheet programs require this for all labels.

4. Generally, if a formula refers to a blank cell or a cell which contains a label, the value of the cell referred to is treated as zero. See a user's manual for specific rules.

5. The number of significant digits maintained in computations varies from one spreadsheet program to another. The number of digits displayed is a function of both the program and the column width being used.

I-3 REPLICATION

One of the features making a spreadsheet program such an excellent tool for implementing mathematical algorithms is its ability to replicate (or repeat) expressions easily. Replication is fundamental to the implementation of most algorithms and examples in this book. Different spreadsheet programs carry this out in different ways. The specific commands of VisiCalc are illustrated here, but the general concepts are applicable to any spreadsheet program. Consult the user's manual for the conventions of a particular spreadsheet program. The descriptive format illustrated in the examples below will be used throughout the book.

Assume that the current content of a spreadsheet is given by Figure I-7. Place the cursor at A2 and enter the command to replicate, /R. A prompt then appears on the screen asking for the locations of the expressions to be replicated and the locations into which the replicated expressions are to be inserted. Enter A2...A2:A3...A6 to indicate that the expression in A2 (literally, the expressions in column A from cell A2 through cell A2) is to be replicated into each cell in column A from

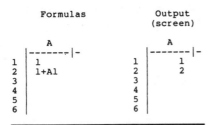

Figure I-7 Current content of spreadsheet.

```
        Formulas              Resulting              Output
                             Spreadsheet            (screen)

          A                      A                      A
     |-------|-              |-------|-             |-------|-
  1  | 1                 1  | 1                 1  |    1
  2  | 1+A1              2  | 1+A1              2  |    2
  3  | |1+A1             3  | 1+A1              3  |    2
  4  | |1+A1             4  | 1+A1              4  |    2
  5  | Replicate         5  | 1+A1              5  |    2
  6  | ↓[N]              6  | 1+A1              6  |    2
```

Figure I-8 Replication: constant [N].

A3 to A6. Another prompt from the computer asks whether the location A1 in the expression 1+A1 is to be treated as a relative location (R) or as a no-change (or constant) location (N).

If N is entered, A1 is treated as a constant location and the expression 1+A1 will be entered unchanged into each of the locations A3, . . . ,A6, as shown in Figure I-8. But if R is entered, A1 is interpreted as a relative location, i.e., "the entry in the location above the current location" (since the A1 appears in an expression in cell A2). This is illustrated in Figure I-9. Note how this operation allows column A to serve as a counter, a construction that will often be used in the book.

It is also possible to replicate expressions and treat some locations as relative and others as constant, as shown in Figure I-10. Note the following convention concerning replication. When an expression in a cell is to be replicated into other cells, an arrow is drawn from the original cell through the cells into which it is to be replicated. A series of N's and R's, one for each variable in the expression, indicates (in order) whether the variables are to be treated as constant (N) or relative (R) locations.

I-4 FUNCTIONS

Each spreadsheet program contains a number of useful library functions. The functions below are all available in VisiCalc, which identifies functions by the initial character @. The evaluation of certain

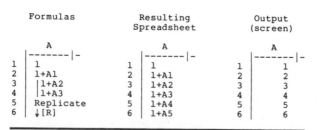

```
        Formulas              Resulting              Output
                             Spreadsheet            (screen)

          A                      A                      A
     |-------|-              |-------|-             |-------|-
  1  | 1                 1  | 1                 1  |    1
  2  | 1+A1              2  | 1+A1              2  |    2
  3  | |1+A2             3  | 1+A2              3  |    3
  4  | |1+A3             4  | 1+A3              4  |    4
  5  | Replicate         5  | 1+A4              5  |    5
  6  | ↓[R]              6  | 1+A5              6  |    6
```

Figure I-9 Replication: relative [R].

functions, especially the exponential, logarithmic, and trigonometric functions, slows the speed of spreadsheet recalculation perceptibly.

Constant Functions

@PI	Returns the value of 3.1415926536
@TRUE, @FALSE	Used with boolean functions
@NA, @ERROR	Not available and error constants

Single-Argument Numerical Functions
(*v* = value)

@SQRT(*v*)	Square root
@ABS(*v*)	Absolute value
@INT(*v*)	Greatest integer
@EXP(*v*)	Exponential (base *e*)
@LOG10(*v*)	Logarithm (base 10)
@LN(*v*)	Logarithm (base *e*)
@SIN(*v*)	Sine*
@COS(*v*)	Cosine*
@TAN(*v*)	Tangent*
@ASIN(*v*)	Arcsine
@ACOS(*v*)	Arccosine
@ATAN(*v*)	Arctangent

* *v* in radians.

Multiple Argument Numerical Functions

(Examples of lists: A1 . . . A8 or A1 . . . K1 or A6, 23, B2)

@MIN(list)	Returns the minimum value in a list
@MAX(list)	Returns the maximum value in a list
@COUNT(list)	Returns the number of values in a list

```
         Formulas              Resulting              Output
                               Spreadsheet            (screen)

           A                      A                      A
    |---------|-           |---------|-           |---------|-
  1 | 2                  1 | 2                   1 |    2
  2 | 3                  2 | 3                   2 |    3
  3 | +A1+A2             3 | +A1+A2              3 |    5
  4 | |+A1+A3            4 | +A1+A3              4 |    7
  5 | |+A1+A4            5 | +A1+A4              5 |    9
  6 | Replicate          6 | +A1+A5              6 |   11
  7 | ↓[NR]              7 | +A1+A6              7 |   13
```

Figure I-10 Replication [NR].

@SUM(list)	Returns the sum of the values in a list
@AVERAGE(list)	Returns the average of the values in a list
@CHOOSE(v,list)	

Example: @CHOOSE(A4,10,9,B6)
Returns 10 if A4 = 1, 9 if A4 = 2, the value of cell B6 if A4= 3, and @NA otherwise

@LOOKUP(v,range)
Suppose that a table of two adjacent columns (rows) has been constructed so that the numbers in a range of cells in the first column (row) are in ascending order. This *table-lookup function* searches for a numerical value v in the first column (row) and returns a value from the second column (row), as illustrated in the following example (See Figure I-11).

Example: @LOOKUP(A6,C10 . . . C12)
Returns 23 if $5 \leqslant$ A6 < 7
$\qquad$ 15 if $7 \leqslant$ A6 < 8
$\qquad$ 81 if A6 $\geqslant 8$
$\qquad$ @NA if A6 < 5
Thus

$$@LOOKUP(8,C10 . . . C12) = 81$$
$$@LOOKUP(7,C10 . . . C12) = 15$$
$$@LOOKUP(6.3,C10 . . . C12) = 23$$
$$@LOOKUP(2,C10 . . . C12) = @NA$$

Boolean Functions (b = boolean expression)

@NOT(b)	Not b
@AND($b1,b2, . . . ,bn$)	b_1 and b_2 and $\cdots$ andb_n
@OR($b1,b2, . . . ,bn$)	b_1 or b_2 or $\cdots$ or b_n
@IF($b,v1,v2$)	If b then v_1, else v_2

Example: @IF(A3 = 5,6,B4)
$\qquad$ If A3 = 5 then 6 is returned
$\qquad\qquad$ else the value of B4 is returned

Exponentiation

The nth power of an expression can be obtained by using the symbol ˆ. For example, +Bl ˆ3 is the cube of the value of cell Bl. This value can be

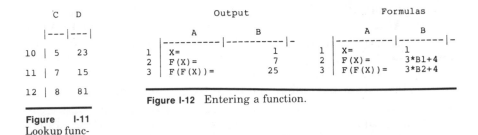

```
      C   D                    Output                        Formulas
   |---|---|                   A         B                   A          B
                          |----------|----------|-      |----------|--------|-
   10 | 5   23         1 | X=           1        1 | X=         1
                       2 | F(X)=        7        2 | F(X)=      3*B1+4
   11 | 7   15         3 | F(F(X))=    25        3 | F(F(X))=   3*B2+4

   12 | 8   81
```

Figure I-12   Entering a function.

Figure   I-11
Lookup func-
tion table.

obtained more rapidly by using +B1*B1*B1. Similarly, a polynomial expression such as $(3*(B1^4))+(5*(B1^3))-(3*B1)+9$ is better written as $+B1*(B1*B1*(3*B1+5)-3)+9$.

User-Defined Functions

User-defined functions are not yet available in most spreadsheet programs. If a function such as $f(x) = 3x + 4$ is to be evaluated, an expression for $f(x)$ must be entered into a particular cell or cells, as shown in Figure I-12.

I-5 CIRCULAR REFERENCE AND RECALCULATION

A recalculation of the spreadsheet can be initiated with the recalculate command (pressing the ! key in VisiCalc). This feature can be used profitably in designing spreadsheets in which a given cell refers to itself either directly or through a circular series of references. Figures I-13 and I-14 illustrate circular reference combined with recalculation.

The use of circular and self-reference is somewhat intricate, each spreadsheet program having its own conventions. The user's manual

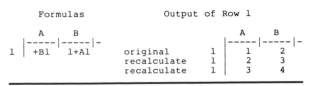

```
       Formulas            Output of Row 1
        A    B                    A   B
    |-----|-----|-          |-----|-----|-
  1 | +B1   1+A1     original      1 | 1   2
                     recalculate   1 | 2   3
                     recalculate   1 | 3   4
```

Figure I-13 Circular reference with recalculation.

should be consulted for details. In Figure I-13 if +Bl is first entered into cell Al of a blank spreadsheet, its value will be 0. If next 1+A1 is entered into cell B1, its value will initially be 1, but as the entire spreadsheet is instantly recalculated the values of cells A1 and B1 will become 1 and 2, respectively. Each time the recalculate command is entered thereafter, the values of A1 and B1 will be modified (increased by 1).

Similarily in Figure I-14 when the expression 1+A1 is entered into cell A1 of a blank spreadsheet, its value is initially 1, but it immediately becomes 2 as the spreadsheet is updated. In each subsequent recalculation the value of cell A1 is increased by 1. Thus, cell A1 almost acts as a counter. The technique shown in Figure I-15, which avoids the initial extra calculation, will be used in a number of implementations in this book. The expression in cell A2 is interpreted

$$\text{If A1} = 0 \text{ then } 1$$
$$\text{else } 1 + \text{A1}$$

Although most of the examples in this book use a separate cell for each computation, the technique of circular reference and recalculation is used in Demonstrations 33 to 36 to create compact spreadsheets which use only a few continually updated cells. Since a spreadsheet has a limited capacity, this technique reduces the number of cells required. In addition, it can often be used to enhance the screen display and to implement a number of additional interactive features.

I-6   DEMONSTRATION FORMAT

The balance of this book contains 36 demonstrations; they describe spreadsheet implementations of mathematical algorithms and provide examples that illustrate mathematical concepts and techniques. These demonstrations are generally presented in the following six-part format.

1. *Algorithm:* The algorithm or concept being illustrated is briefly discussed. In most cases it is assumed that the reader has some

```
        Formulas              Output of Row 1

          A                                A
     |------|-                        |------|-
  1  |  1+A1                original   1  |    2
                           recalculate  1  |    3
                           recalculate  1  |    4
```

Figure I-14   Self-referencing with recalculation.

familiarity with either the algorithm or the setting in which it arises.

2. *Spreadsheet implementation:* Figures display the spreadsheet formulas in a table format, together with sample output (because there is no standard for precision among spreadsheet programs, the exact output will differ with the version). Longer formulas may be listed in the figure below the table. The symbols (R) or (C) indicate the order of recalculation to be used (row by row or column by column). Most examples have been designed for row-by-row recalculation.

3. *Spreadsheet construction:* The steps in constructing the demonstration spreadsheet are outlined, along with an indication of their relationship to the mathematical example.

4. *User interaction:* Ways to exploit the spreadsheet's ability to handle what-if questions are suggested.

5. *Exercises and modifications:* These feature mathematical exercises based on the demonstration spreadsheet, suggestions for modifications or extensions of the spreadsheet, and additional algorithms and examples for which new spreadsheets can be created. Challenging exercises are starred.

6. *References:* Here we list specific numbered references at the end of the book that discuss and develop the algorithms and give examples of their applications.

The mathematical background required for different demonstrations is varied. Many demonstrations, even some, like Demonstration 36, which illustrate advanced topics can be understood by people with no more than advanced high school mathematics, but some demonstrations are obviously designed primarily for people with previous experience in calculus (Demonstrations 5 to 10), numerical analysis (Demonstration 11), linear algebra (Demonstrations 14, 15, and 35), statistics (Demonstrations 23 and 24), linear programming (Demonstrations 30 and 31), and game theory (Demonstration 32). Demonstrations 7 and 9 specifically require the use of calculus, and Demonstrations 30 and 31 are considerably more complex than the others.

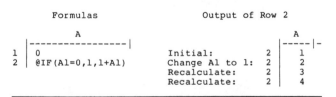
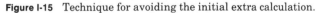

Figure I-15 Technique for avoiding the initial extra calculation.

I-7   ADDITIONAL FEATURES

In addition to the features mentioned above, spreadsheet programs contain many others enabling the user to be creative in constructing a spreadsheet and displaying it on the screen. It is possible to insert, move, or delete rows and columns; to scroll the screen while holding certain rows or columns fixed; to increase or decrease column width in order to increase the number of significant digits in the display or to increase the number of columns shown; to change the order of recalculation from row by row to column by column and vice versa; to use various formats to display the output; and to generate a split screen (or window) to show two nonadjacent sections of the spreadsheet. Exploiting these features, along with headings, user instructions, and other documentation in the spreadsheet, can greatly enhance the output.

To simplify presentation of the mathematical part of the spreadsheet implementations, many of these screen-formatting techniques have been left to the reader. Details can be found in sources listed in section B of the References. In a few of the demonstrations the use of a split screen or window is denoted by //////.

When you have finished with a spreadsheet on the computer, be sure to save it for future use. Instructions for saving can be found in your user's manual.

Fibonacci Numbers

The sequence of Fibonacci numbers, $1, 1, 2, 3, 5, 8, 13, 21, 34, 55, \ldots$, is defined recursively by the relation

$$a_1 = 1, \ a_2 = 1, \ a_n = a_{n-2} + a_{n-1} \qquad n > 2$$

The many intriguing properties of this sequence have fascinated mathematicians for centuries. The sequence appears in a wide variety of applications, including population modeling, the solution of diophantine equations, and the study of the reflection of light [31].

The ratios of successive terms of the sequence have the following property:

$$\lim_{n \to \infty} \frac{a_{n+1}}{a_n} = \frac{\sqrt{5} + 1}{2} \approx 1.618034$$

This number, called the *golden ratio,* arises in the study of proportion in geometry, art, architecture, and biology [31]. If one of the initial terms is changed, the recurrence relation generates another Fibonacci-like sequence ($a_1 = 1$, $a_2 = 3$ gives the Lucas numbers) but the limit remains unchanged.

In Figure 1-1 the Fibonacci numbers are generated using the recurrence relation, and the ratios of successive terms are calculated to illustrate the limit.

SPREADSHEET CONSTRUCTION

1. Enter the initial terms of the Fibonacci sequence, $a_1 = 1$ and $a_2 = 1$, into cells A5 and A6.

2. Enter the formula for a_3, +A5+A6, into cell A7. To produce $a_n = a_{n-2} + a_{n-1}$ for $n = 4, 5, 6, \ldots$ replicate this expression down column A, with both locations relative.

3. Enter the quotient of the first two terms of the Fibonacci sequence, +A6/A5, into cell B6 and replicate (column B).

USER INTERACTION

Change the values of a_1 and a_2 (cells A5 and A6). This generates sequences which are similar to the sequence of Fibonacci numbers. Notice that for any choice of a_1 and a_2 $\lim\limits_{n \to \infty} (a_{n+1}/a_n)$ remains unchanged.

Exercises and Modifications

1-1. Modify the basic spreadsheet by including a column which counts the terms of the sequence.

1-2. Create spreadsheets to generate the sequences defined by the following relations (see Ref. 58 for a discussion of recursively defined sequences and applications which give rise to similar recurrence relations):

a. Arithmetic sequence:

$$a_1 = 50, a_n = a_{n-1} + 200, \text{ for } n > 1$$

b. Geometric sequence (money at 6% annual interest):

$$a_1 = 500, a_n = 1.06a_{n-1}, \text{ for } n > 1$$

c. Money at 6% annual interest with annual $200 deposits:

$$a_1 = 500, a_n = 1.06a_{n-1} + 200, \text{ for } n > 1$$

```
               Output                        Formulas (R)

           A          B                    A           B
      |----------|----------|-        |----------|-----------|-
   1  | FIBONACCI  NUMBERS       1    | FIBONACCI  NUMBERS
   2  |                         2    |
   3  | FIB.NO.    RATIO        3    | FIB.NO.    RATIO
   4  |                         4    |
   5  |    1                    5    | 1
   6  |    1          1         6    | 1          +A6/A5
   7  |    2          2         7    | +A5+A6    |+A7/A6
   8  |    3         1.5        8    ||+A6+A7    |+A8/A7
   9  |    5      1.666667      9    ||+A7+A8    |+A9/A8
   :  |                         :    ||   :      |   :
      |                              ||Replicate  Replicate
      |                              ||[RR]      |[RR]
   :  |                         :    ||   :      |   :
  22  |  2584     1.618034     22    ||+A20+A21  |+A22/A21
  23  |  4181     1.618034     23    |↓+A21+A22  ↓+A23/A22
```

Figure 1-1 Fibonacci numbers.

d. $a_1 = 1$, $a_2 = 2$, $a_{n+2} = -a_n + 2a_{n+1}$, for $n > 0$

e. $a_0 = a_1 = 1$, $a_2 = 3$, $a_{n+3} = 3a_{n+2} - 2a_{n+1} + a_n$, for $n \geqslant 0$

1-3. Create a spreadsheet to find the square root of N using the well-known elementary algorithm

$$a_1 = \text{guess} \qquad a_{n+1} = 0.5\left(a_n + \frac{N}{a_n}\right) \qquad n > 0$$

This is a special case of Newton's method (see Demonstration 7).

1-4. The Fibonacci numbers have many interesting properties [12, 29, 31]. For example,

$$a_1^2 + a_2^2 + \cdots + a_n^2 = a_n a_{n+1}$$

Modify the basic spreadsheet and investigate this property.

REFERENCES

Fibonacci numbers: references 8, 12, 16, 29, 31, 33, and 39.

Recurrence relations (difference equations): references 8, 16, 18, 27, 38, and 58.

Square-root algorithm: references 9, 21, and 52.

Factorials

For a positive integer n, $n!$ (read "n factorial") is defined recursively by

$$1! = 1 \qquad n! = n(n - 1)! \qquad \text{for } n > 1$$

or equivalently,

$$a_1 = 1 \qquad a_n = na_{n-1} \qquad \text{for } n > 1$$

Thus

$$4! = 4 \cdot 3! = 4 \cdot 3 \cdot 2! = 4 \cdot 3 \cdot 2 \cdot 1$$

These expressions occur in all fields of mathematics, especially in combinatorics, probability, and calculus. The spreadsheet in Figure 2-1 uses the recurrence relation to generate $n!$.

SPREADSHEET CONSTRUCTION

1. Column A serves as a counter. Enter 1 into cell A5, 1+A5 into cell A6, and replicate (column A).

2. Values of $n!$ are generated in column B. Since $1! = 1$, enter +A5 into cell B5. Each subsequent entry in column B is the product of the current value of n (the cell to the left) and $(n - 1)!$ (the cell above). Enter +A6*B5 into cell B6 and replicate (column B).

Exercises and Modifications

2-1. The number of regions in a plane created by n mutually intersecting circles no three of which have a common intersection point is given by [38, p. 59]

$$a_1 = 2 \qquad a_n = a_{n-1} + 2(n - 1) \qquad \text{for } n > 1$$

Create a spreadsheet to implement this recurrence relation.

2-2. The probability that in a group of n people no two will have the same birthday (neglecting February 29) is given by

$$P_n = \frac{365}{365} \cdot \frac{364}{365} \cdot \frac{363}{365} \cdots \cdots \frac{366 - n}{365}$$

P_n can be defined recursively by

$$P_1 = 1, \qquad P_n = \frac{P_{n-1}(366 - n)}{365} \qquad \text{for } n > 1$$

Create a spreadsheet to find $1 - P_n$, the probability [33] that in a group of n people at least two have the same birthday, for $n = 1, 2, 3, \ldots$.

2-3. The factorial spreadsheet also illustrates a double-subscripted recurrence relation

$$a_{1,1} = a_{1,2} = 1, \; a_{n,1} = a_{n-1,1} + 1, \; a_{n,2} = a_{n,1}a_{n-1,2} \qquad \text{for } n > 1$$

Create a spreadsheet to generate Pascal's triangle using the recurrence relation

$$a_{n,1} = 1 \qquad \text{for } n > 0$$
$$a_{1,k} = 0 \qquad \text{for } k > 1$$
$$a_{n,k} = a_{n-1,k-1} + a_{n-1,k} \qquad \text{for } n > 1 \text{ and } k > 1$$

(see Demonstration 18).

2-4. Read Ref. 31 or 37 for a discussion of figurate (polynomial) numbers. Create spreadsheets to generate some of these numbers.

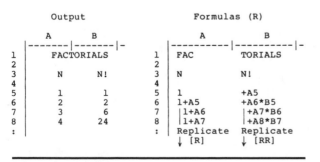

	Output			Formulas (R)	
	A	B		A	B
1	FACTORIALS		1	FAC	TORIALS
2			2		
3	N	N!	3	N	N!
4			4		
5	1	1	5	1	+A5
6	2	2	6	1+A5	+A6*B5
7	3	6	7	1+A6	+A7*B6
8	4	24	8	1+A7	+A8*B7
:			:	Replicate ↓ [R]	Replicate ↓ [RR]

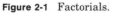

Figure 2-1 Factorials.

REFERENCES

Factorials: references 8, 16, 19, 27, 34, and 50.

Recurrence relations (difference equations): references 8, 16, 18, 27, 38, and 58.

Figurate (polynomial) numbers: references 7, 21, 31, 37, and 52.

Pascal's triangle: references 8, 12, 16, 33, and 58.

Birthday problem: references 27 and 33.

Bisection Algorithm

The bisection algorithm is a standard method of locating the zeros of a continuous function. Let $[a_0, b_0]$ be an interval in which $f(a_0)$ and $f(b_0)$ have opposite signs; that is, $f(a_0)f(b_0) < 0$, so that f has a zero in the interval. Let $m_0 = 0.5 (a_0 + b_0)$ be the midpoint of the interval. Define a second interval $[a_1, b_1]$ as either $[a_0, m_0]$ or $[m_0, b_0]$. Now

$$\text{If } f(a_0)f(m_0) \leq 0 \text{ then } a_1 = a_0 \text{ and } b_1 = m_0$$
$$\text{else } a_1 = m_0 \text{ and } b_1 = b_0$$

Now f has a zero in $[a_1, b_1]$. Repeat the process. In general, once the interval $[a_n, b_n]$ has been determined, $[a_{n+1}, b_{n+1}]$ will be given by

$$\text{If } f(a_0)f(m_n) \leq 0 \text{ then } a_{n+1} = a_n \text{ and } b_{n+1} = m_n$$
$$\text{else } a_{n+1} = m_n \text{ and } b_{n+1} = b_n$$

where $m_n = 0.5(a_n + b_n)$. The sequence $m_0, m_1, m_2, \ldots$ converges to a zero of f.

This algorithm is illustrated in Figure 3-1 and implemented in Figure 3-2 using the function $f(x) = x^2 - 2$. The initial interval $[a_0, b_0]$ is entered by the user. In the spreadsheet $[a_0, b_0] = [1, 2]$, and the midpoints converge to $\sqrt{2}$. This algorithm can be improved if one of the m_n's itself a zero of f (see Exercise 3-1).

SPREADSHEET CONSTRUCTION

1. Enter the endpoints of the initial interval into cells B4 and D4 and copy them into cells A7 and B7.

2. Compute the midpoint of the first interval in cell C7 [.5*(A7+B7)], evaluate the function at the midpoint in cell D7 (+C7*C7−2), and replicate (columns C and D).

3. If the function changes signs on the left half interval, the new left endpoint is the previous left endpoint (A7); otherwise it is the previous midpoint (C7). Enter

$$@IF((A7*A7−2)*(C7*C7−2)<=0,A7,C7)$$

into cell A8 and replicate (column A).

4. If the left endpoint remains unchanged in successive iterations, the right endpoint of the new interval is the previous midpoint (C7); otherwise it is the previous right endpoint (B7). Enter

$$@IF(A8=A7,C7,B7)$$

into cell B8 and replicate (column B).

USER INTERACTION

1. Change the initial interval (B4, D4).

2. Change the function by changing the expressions in cells D7 and A8 and replicating (columns D and A).

Exercises and Modifications

3-1. If one of the m_n's is a root of f, the iterations can be terminated. Modify the spreadsheet by changing the expressions in cells A8 and B8 to

$$@IF(D7=0,A7,\text{———}) \quad \text{and} \quad @IF(D7=0,B7,\text{———})$$

respectively, and replicating (columns A and B). The blank represents the current entry in each cell. Find a zero of $f(x) = x^2 − 2.25$ using [1, 5] as the initial interval with both the original and modified algorithms. Remember to change the function in columns A and D.

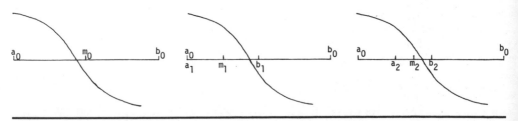

Figure 3-1 Bisection algorithm.

3-2. Modify the spreadsheet to locate the three roots of

$$f(x) = x^3 + 15x^2 - 109x + 132 = x[x(x + 15) - 109] + 132$$

3-3. Modify the spreadsheet to locate the roots of the function

$$f(x) = x^3 - 21x^2 + 11x - 1$$

Begin with B4 = 0 and D4 = 1. Then try B4 = 0.1 and D4 = 0.2. Find all three roots. ●

3-4. Modify the spreadsheet so that a_0 and the width of the initial interval are parameters and b_0 is computed. Repeat Exercise 3-3 using the modified spreadsheet.

3-5. Add a counter column to the spreadsheet. Observe the rate of convergence of the bisection algorithm and compare it with Newton's method (Demonstration 7) using the same function.

3-6. The method of *false position* is similar to the bisection algorithm. If $f(a_n)$ and $f(b_n)$ have opposite signs, let x_n denote the x intercept of the line connecting the points $(a_n, f(a_n))$ and $(b_n, f(b_n))$. If $f(x_n)f(a_n) < 0$, set $a_{n+1} = a_n$ and $b_{n+1} = x_n$; otherwise set $a_{n+1} = x_n$

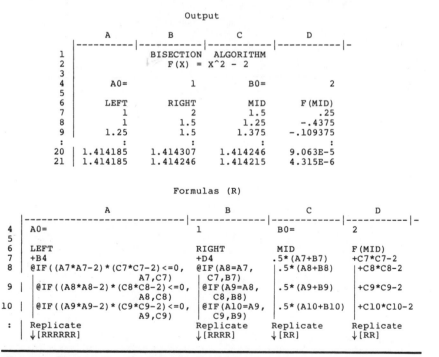

Output

	A	B	C	D
1		BISECTION	ALGORITHM	
2		F(X)	= X^2 - 2	
3				
4	A0=	1	B0=	2
5				
6	LEFT	RIGHT	MID	F(MID)
7	1	2	1.5	.25
8	1	1.5	1.25	-.4375
9	1.25	1.5	1.375	-.109375
:	:	:	:	:
20	1.414185	1.414307	1.414246	9.063E-5
21	1.414185	1.414246	1.414215	4.315E-6

Formulas (R)

	A	B	C	D
4	A0=	1	B0=	2
5				
6	LEFT	RIGHT	MID	F(MID)
7	+B4	+D4	.5*(A7+B7)	+C7*C7-2
8	@IF((A7*A7-2)*(C7*C7-2)<=0, A7,C7)	@IF(A8=A7, C7,B7)	.5*(A8+B8)	+C8*C8-2
9	@IF((A8*A8-2)*(C8*C8-2)<=0, A8,C8)	@IF(A9=A8, C8,B8)	.5*(A9+B9)	+C9*C9-2
10	@IF((A9*A9-2)*(C9*C9-2)<=0, A9,C9)	@IF(A10=A9, C9,B9)	.5*(A10+B10)	+C10*C10-2
:	Replicate ↓[RRRRRR]	Replicate ↓[RRRR]	Replicate ↓[RR]	Replicate ↓[RR]

Figure 3-2 The bisection algorithm for $f(x) = x^2 - 2$.

and $b_{n+1} = b_n$. Under suitable conditions [11, p. 42] the sequence $x_1, x_2, x_3, \ldots$ converges to a root of $y = f(x)$. Design a spreadsheet for the method of false position and locate the roots of $f(x) = x^2 - 2$ [note that $x_n = (2 + a_n b_n)/(a_n + b_n)$]. Use $a_0 = 1$, $b_0 = 2$.

REFERENCES

Bisection algorithm: references 5, 11, 17, 22, 23, 30, and 59.

False position: references 5, 11, 17, 22, 23, 59, and 61.

Fixed-Point Algorithm

A fixed point of a function $y = g(x)$ is a number p for which $g(p) = p$. For example, -2 and 3 are fixed points of $g(x) = x^2 - 6$ since $g(-2) = -2$ and $g(3) = 3$. Graphically, a fixed point p of $y = g(x)$ corresponds to a point where the graph of $y = g(x)$ and the line $y = x$ intersect. Clearly, not all functions have fixed points. For example, if $g(x) = x + 1$, there is no point p for which $p = g(p) = p + 1$.

An iterative algorithm for finding a fixed point of $y = g(x)$ is given by obtaining an initial estimate x_0 for p and forming a sequence

$$x_0, x_1 = g(x_0), x_2 = g(x_1), \ldots, x_n = g(x_{n-1}), \ldots$$

Under suitable conditions [11, pp. 26–32] the sequence converges to a point p, which must be a fixed point of g. This algorithm is illustrated in Figure 4-1 and implemented in the spreadsheet in Figure 4-2.

A fixed point of $y = g(x)$ is also a zero of $f(x) = x - g(x)$ since $f(p) = p - g(p) = 0$. It is often possible to find a zero of a function $y = f(x)$ by finding a fixed point of a related function. For example, if p is a zero of $f(x) = x^3 + 5x^2 - 8$, then $p^3 + 5p^2 - 8 = 0$; therefore

$$p^3 + 5p^2 = 8 \qquad p^2 = \frac{8}{p + 5} \qquad p = \sqrt{\frac{8}{p + 5}}$$

and p is a fixed point of $g(x) = \sqrt{8/(x + 5)}$. This function is used with the fixed-point algorithm in the spreadsheet (Figure 4-2). Unfortunately, the algorithm does not converge for every function g derived from a function f (see Exercise 4-4).

Finally, note that Newton's method (Demonstration 7) locates a zero of $f(x)$ by finding a fixed point of $g(x) = x - f(x)/f'(x)$ using this algorithm [see part (g) of Exercise 4-4].

SPREADSHEET CONSTRUCTION

1. Enter the initial estimate x_0 of a fixed point into cell B4 and copy it (+B4) into cell B7.
2. The expression for $x_1 = g(x_0)$ is @SQRT(8/(5+B7)). Enter it into cell B8. Compute $x_2 = g(x_1)$, $x_3 = g(x_2)$, . . . by replicating the expression in cell B8 down column B, with the variable relative.
3. Use column A as a counter. Enter 0 into cell A7 and 1+A7 into cell A8 and replicate the latter expression down column A, with the variable relative.

USER INTERACTION

1. Vary the initial approximation x_0 (B4). Observe the rate of convergence (or notice divergence) and the fixed point to which the algorithm converges.
2. Change the function in cell B8 and replicate the new expression down column B.

Exercises and Modifications

4-1. Modify the spreadsheet to find a fixed point of the function $g(x) =$ cos $(\pi x/180)$. Start from $x_0 = 0$. Note the rapid convergence. Carry

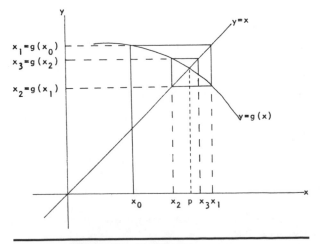

Figure 4-1 Fixed-point algorithm.

	Output			Formulas (R)		
	A	B		A	B	
1	FIXED-POINT		1	FIXED-	POINT	
2	G(X)=SQRT(8/(5+X))		2	G(X)=SQR	T(8/5+X))	
3			3			
4	INIT X	1	4	INIT X	1	
5			5			
6	COUNT	G(X)	6	COUNT	G(X)	
7	0	1	7	0	+B4	
8	1	1.154701	8	1+A7	@SQRT(8/(5+B7))	
9	2	1.140096	9	1+A8	@SQRT(8/(5+B8))	
10	3	1.141451	10	1+A9	@SQRT(8/(5+B9))	
:	:	:	:	:	:	
14	7	1.141336	14	Replicate	Replicate	
15	8	1.141336	15	↓[R]	↓[R]	

Figure 4-2 Fixed-point algorithm for $g(x) = \sqrt{8/(5 + x)}$.

this out on a hand calculator in degree mode by entering 0 and repeatedly pressing the COS key.

4-2. Repeat Exercise 4-1 using $g(x) - \cos x$ and note the slow convergence. Carry this out on a hand calculator in radian mode by entering 0 and repeatedly pressing the COS key.

4-3. Investigate the convergence of the fixed-point algorithm for the functions $g(x) = (\exp x + x^2)/k$, using various values of k. Treat k as a parameter. Use $x_0 = 0$.

4-4. Let $f(x) = x^3 + 5x^2 - 8$. Derive each of the following functions $g(x)$ from $f(x)$ by simple algebraic manipulations. Examine each for fixed points, which will also be roots of $f(x)$. Not all will converge. Notice that part g is Newton's method (see Demonstration 7).

a. $g(x) = x - x^3 - 5x^2 + 8$

b. $g(x) = \sqrt{\dfrac{8}{x} - 5x}$

c. $g(x) = \sqrt{\dfrac{8 - x^3}{5}}$

d. $g(x) = \sqrt{\dfrac{8}{5 + x}}$

e. $g(x) = \sqrt[3]{8 - 5x^2}$

f. $g(x) = \dfrac{8 - x^3}{5x}$

g. $g(x) = x - \dfrac{x^3 + 5x^2 - 8}{3x^2 + 10x}$

REFERENCES

Fixed-point algorithm: references 5, 11, 23, 59, and 61.

Newton's method: references 5, 11, 17, 22, 23, 28, 30, 43, 55, and 59.

Limits

The concept of a limit is fundamental to calculus. Intuitively, the expression $\lim_{x \to a} f(x) = L$ can be interpreted to mean that $f(x)$ will be arbitrarily close to L if x is chosen sufficiently close to a (see Figure 5-1).

An equivalent expression is given by

$$L = \lim_{x \to a} f(x) = \lim_{h \to 0} f(a + h)$$

The spreadsheet (Figure 5-2) calculates $f(a + h)$ for small values of h, both positive and negative, as the approximation of the limit. The user can enter the value of a, as well as an initial value h_0 for h. Additional values of h are generated by using a reduction factor r $(0 < r < 1)$:

$$h_1 = rh_0, \ h_2 = rh_1, \ \ldots$$

The spreadsheet (Figure 5-2) uses

$$f(x) = \frac{\sin x}{|x|}$$

The output with $a = 0$ suggests that $\lim_{x \to 0} f(x)$ does not exist and that $\lim_{x \to 0^+} f(x) = 1$ and $\lim_{x \to 0^-} f(x) = -1$. However, when $a = 0.01$, the output suggests that $\lim_{x \to a} f(x) \approx 0.9999833$.

This intuitive technique can sometimes be misleading if care is not taken in the choice of h [see part (e) Exercise 5-1]. Reference 47 discusses limits and formal methods of verifying that the observed estimates are indeed correct.

SPREADSHEET CONSTRUCTION

1. Enter a, h_0, and the reduction factor r into cells B5, B6, and B7.
2. Generate values of h modified by the reduction factor as shown in cells A10 to A24. Note that in cells A11 to A15 each entry equals B7 times the previous h; in cells A20 to A24 each entry equals the previous h divided by cell B7.
3. Evaluate $a + h$ in column B by entering +B5+A10 into cell B10 and replicating (column B).
4. Evaluate $f(a + h)$ in column C by entering @SIN(B10)/@ABS(B10) into cell C10 and replicating (column C).

USER INTERACTION

1. Vary the value of a in cell B5 to approximate limits at points $x = a$.
2. Change the initial h_0 in cell B6 and the reduction factor r in cell B7 to examine the value of $f(x)$ at other points x approaching a.

Exercises and Modifications

5-1. Use the spreadsheet to investigate the following limits:

a. $\lim\limits_{x \to 0} \dfrac{|x|}{x}$ b. $\lim\limits_{x \to 0.01} \dfrac{|x|}{x}$

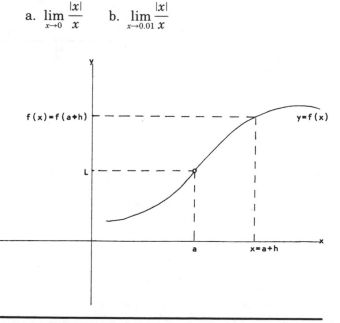

Figure 5-1 Limits.

c. $\lim\limits_{x\to 0} \dfrac{\sin x}{x}$ d. $\lim\limits_{x\to 0} \dfrac{\sin 5x}{3x}$

e. $\lim\limits_{x\to 0} \cos \dfrac{\pi}{x}$ f. $\lim\limits_{x\to 3} \dfrac{x^2 - 9}{x - 3}$

5-2. Evaluate the following limits, which arise in the study of the

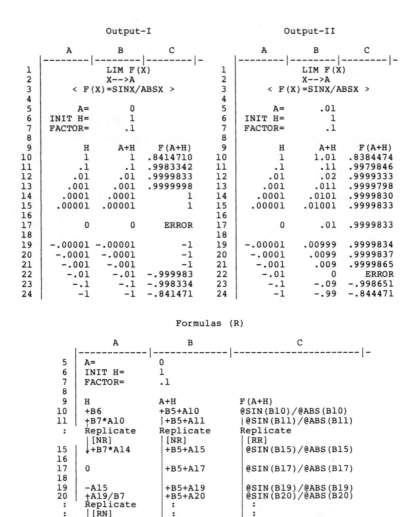

```
                Output-I                            Output-II

          A        B        C                 A        B        C
    |--------|--------|--------|-        |--------|--------|--------|-
 1  |         LIM F(X)                1  |         LIM F(X)
 2  |          X-->A                  2  |          X-->A
 3  |     < F(X)=SINX/ABSX >          3  |     < F(X)=SINX/ABSX >
 4  |                                 4  |
 5  |     A=        0                 5  |     A=       .01
 6  | INIT H=       1                 6  | INIT H=       1
 7  | FACTOR=      .1                 7  | FACTOR=      .1
 8  |                                 8  |
 9  |     H       A+H     F(A+H)      9  |     H       A+H     F(A+H)
10  |     1        1    .8414710     10  |     1      1.01    .8384474
11  |    .1       .1    .9983342     11  |    .1       .11    .9979846
12  |   .01      .01    .9999833     12  |   .01      .02    .9999333
13  |  .001     .001    .9999998     13  |  .001     .011    .9999798
14  | .0001    .0001        1        14  | .0001    .0101    .9999830
15  |.00001   .00001        1        15  |.00001   .01001    .9999833
16  |                                16  |
17  |    0        0      ERROR       17  |    0       .01    .9999833
18  |                                18  |
19  |-.00001  -.00001      -1        19  |-.00001   .00999    .9999834
20  | -.0001   -.0001      -1        20  | -.0001    .0099    .9999837
21  |  -.001    -.001      -1        21  |  -.001     .009    .9999865
22  |   -.01     -.01   -.999983     22  |   -.01       0      ERROR
23  |    -.1      -.1   -.998334     23  |    -.1      -.09  -.998651
24  |     -1       -1   -.841471     24  |     -1      -.99  -.844471
```

```
                        Formulas (R)

             A                    B                     C
    |---------------|---------------|-----------------------|-
 5  | A=             0
 6  | INIT H=        1
 7  | FACTOR=       .1
 8  |
 9  | H              A+H             F(A+H)
10  | +B6            +B5+A10         @SIN(B10)/@ABS(B10)
11  | +B7*A10       |+B5+A11        |@SIN(B11)/@ABS(B11)
 :  | Replicate      Replicate       Replicate
    | |[NR]          |[NR]           [RR]
15  |↓+B7*A14        +B5+A15         @SIN(B15)/@ABS(B15)
16  |
17  | 0              +B5+A17         @SIN(B17)/@ABS(B17)
18  |
19  | -A15           +B5+A19         @SIN(B19)/@ABS(B19)
20  | +A19/B7        +B5+A20         @SIN(B20)/@ABS(B20)
 :  | Replicate       :               :
 :  | |[RN]           :               :
24  |↓+A23/B7        ↓+B5+A24        ↓@SIN(B24)/@ABS(B24)
```

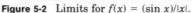

Figure 5-2 Limits for $f(x) = (\sin x)/|x|$.

exponential function [43]:

a. $\lim_{x \to 0} (1 + x)^{1/x}$ b. $\lim_{x \to 0} (1 + rx)^{1/x}$, $r = 0.05, 0.1$

5-3. Create a spreadsheet to investigate

$$f'(a) = \lim_{h \to 0} \frac{f(a + h) - f(a)}{h}$$

See also Demonstration 6.

REFERENCES

Limits: references 2, 22, 43, 50, 55, and 63

Differentiation

One of the basic concepts of calculus is that of the derivative. The derivative $f'(a)$ of a function f evaluated at $x = a$ is given by

$$f'(a) = \lim_{h \to 0} \frac{f(a + h) - f(a)}{h}$$

provided that the limit exists. Geometrically, $f'(a)$ is the slope of the line tangent to the curve $y = f(x)$ at the point $x = a$. For small h, $f'(a)$ can be approximated by the difference quotient $[f(a + h) - f(a)]/h$ (see Figure 6-1).

The spreadsheet for estimating $f'(a)$ is a modification of the limit spreadsheet for Demonstration 5. The user enters an initial value h_0 for h; additional values for h are generated by the use of a reduction factor r $(0 < r < 1)$: $h_1 = rh_0$, $h_2 = rh_1$, . . . ; and corresponding values for $[f(a + h) - f(a)]/h$ are calculated as approximations for $f'(a)$. Theoretically, answers will improve as h approaches 0. However, if h becomes too small, roundoff errors in calculations will cause the accuracy of the estimate to deteriorate.

The spreadsheet (Figure 6-2) suggests that if $f(x) = x^2$, then $f'(3) = \lim_{h \to 0} [f(3 + h) - f(3)]/h \approx 6$.

SPREADSHEET CONSTRUCTION

1. Enter a, h_0, and a reduction factor r into cells B5, B6, and B7 and enter +B5*B5, the expression for $f(a)$, into cell D5.

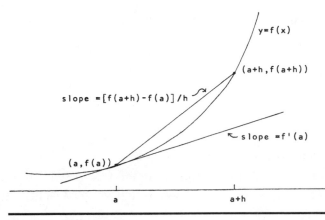

Figure 6-1 Differentiation.

```
                              Output

                A        B        C        D
        |---------|----------|-----------|-----------|-
   1              DIFFERENCE  QUOTIENT
   2                F(X)  =  X^2
   3
   4
   5        A=          3    F(A)=           9
   6    INIT H=         1
   7    FACTOR=        .1
   8
   9        H          A+H    F(A+H)    DIFF QUO
  10        1           4      16          7
  11       .1          3.1     9.61        6.1
  12       .01         3.01    9.0601      6.01
  13       .001        3.001   9.006001    6.001
  14       .0001       3.0001  9.000600    6.0001
  15       .00001      3.00001 9.000060    6.00001
  16
  17        0           3       9
  18
  19     -.00001       2.99999  8.999940    5.99999
  20     -.0001        2.9999   8.999400    5.9999
  21     -.001         2.999    8.994001    5.999
  22     -.01          2.99     8.9401      5.99
  23     -.1           2.9      8.41        5.9
  24     -1            2        4           5
```

```
                           Formulas (R)

             A            B            C            D
       |-------------|-------------|------------|----------------|-
   5   A=            3             F(A)=        +B5*B5
   6   INIT H=       1
   7   FACTOR=       .1
   8
   9   H             A+H           F(A+H)       DIFF QUO
  10   +B6           +B5+A10       +B10*B10     (C10-D5)/A10
  11   +B7*A10       +B5+A11       +B11*B11     (C11-D5)/A11
  12   +B7*A11       +B5+A12       +B12*B12     (C12-D5)/A12
   :   [copy from    Replicate     Replicate    Replicate
   :     Demo. 5]    [NR]          [RR]          [RNR]
  24   +A23/B7       +B5+A24       +B24*B24     (C24-D5)/A24
```

Enter blanks into cells B,C:16,18 and D:16-18.

Figure 6-2 Differentiation for $f(x) = x^2$.

2. Complete columns A, B, and C as in Demonstration 5.
3. Calculate the difference quotient $[f(a + h) - f(a)]/h$ in column D. Enter (C10-D5)/A10 into cell D10 and replicate (column D).

USER INTERACTION

1. Evaluate $f'(a)$ for various values of a (cell B5).
2. Change the initial h_0 (cell B6) or the reduction factor r (cell B7) to examine the difference quotient for additional points x approaching a.

Exercises and Modifications

6-1. Estimate $f'(a)$ for the following functions and values of a:
   a. $f(x) = x^5$, $a = 1, 2, 3, \ldots$ b. $f(x) = x^4 + 5x - 7$, $a = 1, 6$
6-2. a. Use a spreadsheet to estimate $f'(a)$ for various a using $f(x) = \sin x$. Include a cell which computes $\cos a$ and compare $\cos a$ with $f'(a)$.
   b. Use a spreadsheet to examine $f'(a)$ for $f(x) = \exp x$. Compare $\exp a$ with $f'(a)$.
6-3. In the example spreadsheet reduce h_0 to values near 1×10^{-5}. What happens to the accuracy of the answer?
6-4. A more precise estimate for the derivative can be found using the formula [11, p. 128]

$$f'(a) \approx \frac{- 3f(a) + 4f(a + h) - f(a + 2h)}{2h}$$

Create a spreadsheet for this algorithm and use it to estimate $f'(0)$, $f'(1.8)$, and $f'(2.19)$ for:
   a. $f(x) = \exp x$ b. $f(x) = x^2 \exp x^2 - \sin x$
   c. $f(x) = \tan x$
   Notice that the accuracy of this algorithm also deteriorates if h is too small. Use values of h_0 near 0.0001 in your spreadsheet for part (a) to find $f'(0)$.
6-5. The central-difference quotient [11, p. 128] is another means of approximating the derivative

$$f'(a) \approx \frac{f(a + h) - f(a - h)}{2h}$$

Design a spreadsheet using this expression.

6-6. One numerical algorithm for finding the second derivative is given by [11, p. 135]

$$f''(a) \approx \frac{f(a - h) - 2f(a) + f(a + h)}{h^2}$$

Create a spreadsheet for this algorithm.

REFERENCES

Derivative: references 2, 43, and 55.

Numerical differentiation: references 11, 22, 23, 30, and 59.

Newton's Method

Newton's method, which employs the concept of the derivative from calculus, is one of the best known and most powerful algorithms for finding a zero of a differentiable function $y = f(x)$. To begin, let x_0 be an approximation of a zero for which $f'(x_0) \neq 0$. The line tangent to $y = f(x)$ at $(x_0, f(x_0))$ is

$$y = f(x_0) + f'(x_0)(x - x_0)$$

This line intersects the x axis at $(x_1, 0)$, where

$$0 = f(x_0) + f'(x_0)(x_1 - x_0) \qquad \text{or} \qquad x_1 = x_0 - \frac{f(x_0)}{f'(x_0)}$$

(see Figure 7-1). The value x_1 is generally a much better approximation of the zero than x_0. This process is now repeated by defining successive approximations x_n using the recurrence relation

$$x_{n+1} = x_n - \frac{f(x_n)}{f'(x_n)}$$

until the desired accuracy is obtained. Reference 17 and Exercises 7-3 and 7-4 give examples for which the sequence does not converge.

The spreadsheet (Figure 7-2) employs the recurrence relation for Newton's method and displays values for x_n, $f(x_n)$, and $f'(x_n)$ using the function $f(x) = 0.1x - \cos x$. The initial estimate x_0 is entered by the user. Notice that with $x_0 = 1$ Newton's method produces a sequence which rapidly converges to 1.427522 as an approximation of a zero. To modify this spreadsheet for another function a user must first calculate the derivative.

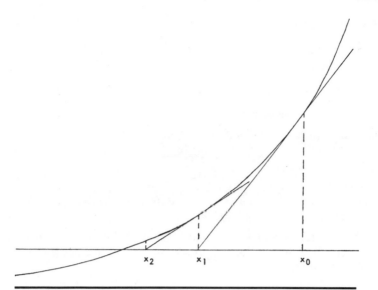

Figure 7-1 Newton's method.

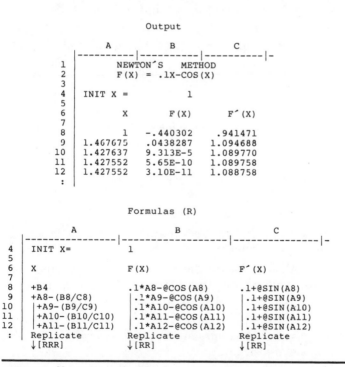

Output

	A	B	C
1	NEWTON'S METHOD		
2	F(X) = .1X-COS(X)		
3			
4	INIT X =	1	
5			
6	X	F(X)	F´(X)
7			
8	1	-.440302	.941471
9	1.467675	.0438287	1.094688
10	1.427637	9.313E-5	1.089770
11	1.427552	5.65E-10	1.089758
12	1.427552	3.10E-11	1.088758
:			

Formulas (R)

	A	B	C
4	INIT X=	1	
5			
6	X	F(X)	F´(X)
7			
8	+B4	.1*A8-@COS(A8)	.1+@SIN(A8)
9	+A8-(B8/C8)	.1*A9-@COS(A9)	.1+@SIN(A9)
10	+A9-(B9/C9)	.1*A10-@COS(A10)	.1+@SIN(A10)
11	+A10-(B10/C10)	.1*A11-@COS(A11)	.1+@SIN(A11)
12	+A11-(B11/C11)	.1*A12-@COS(A12)	.1+@SIN(A12)
:	Replicate	Replicate	Replicate
	↓[RRR]	↓[RR]	↓[RR]

Figure 7-2 Newton's method for $f(x) = 0.1x - \cos x$, $f'(x) = 0.1^+\sin x$.

SPREADSHEET CONSTRUCTION

1. Enter the initial approximation x_0 of the zero into cell B4 and copy
   this value into cell A8. Enter

   $$.1*A8 - @COS(A8) \qquad \text{and} \qquad .1 + @SIN(A8)$$

   into cells B8 and C8, respectively, to evaluate $f(x_0)$ and $f'(x_0)$.

2. Enter the expression $+A8 - (B8/C8)$ into cell A9 to calculate

   $$x_1 = x_0 - \frac{f'(x_0)}{f(x_0)}$$

   To compute subsequent values of x_n replicate this expression down
   column A, with all locations relative.

3. Values of the function and its derivative are calculated in columns
   B and C, respectively, by replicating the expressions in cells B8 and
   C8 (columns B and C).

USER INTERACTION

1. Enter various values for x_0 into cell B4 to find other zeros of $y = f(x)$.

2. Change the expressions for $f(x)$ and $f'(x)$ in cells B8 and C8 and
   replicate them down columns B and C to find zeros of other functions.

Exercises and Modifications

7-1. Vary x_0 (cell B4) and locate all the zeros of $f(x) = 0.1x - \cos x$.
     Notice that both the zero located and the rate of convergence of
     the algorithm are influenced by the choice of x_0.

7-2. Modify the spreadsheet for Newton's method to locate the zeros:
     a. $f(x) = x^2 - 2$ (see also Exercise 1-3)
     b. $f(x) = x^3 + 15x^2 - 109x + 132$

7-3. Use Newton's method to locate the zeros of $f(x) = -2x^3 + 3x^2 + x - 1$.
     Observe what happens when $x_0 = 0$ or 1.

7-4. Use Newton's method to locate the zero of $f(x) = (4x-3)/(x-1)$.
     Notice how sensitive the algorithm is to the choice of x_0. Investi-
     gate the result of using $x_0 = -1$, 0, 0.49, 0.5, 0.51, 0.7, 0.75, 0.99,
     and 1.

7-5. Add a counter column to the spreadsheet and observe the rate of
     convergence of the algorithm.

7-6. The *secant method* [11] is an algorithm similar to Newton's method for approximating zeros. If x_1 and x_2 are two initial approximations of a zero of $y = f(x)$, define x_3 by

$$x_3 = x_2 - \frac{f(x_2)(x_2 - x_1)}{f(x_2) - f(x_1)}$$

and x_n for $n > 2$ by

$$x_n = x_{n-1} - \frac{f(x_{n-1})(x_{n-1} - x_{n-2})}{f(x_{n-1}) - f(x_{n-2})}$$

Under suitable conditions the sequence $x_1, x_2, x_3, \ldots$ converges to a zero of $f(x)$. Design a spreadsheet for the secant method and use it to locate the zeros of $f(x) = x^3 - 3x^2 + 5$.

REFERENCES

Newton's method: references 5, 11, 17, 22, 23, 28, 30, 43, 55, 59, and 61.

Secant method: references 5, 11, 22, 23, 30, 59, and 61.

Demonstration

8

Numerical Integration
Trapezoidal Rule
and Simpson's Rule

The trapezoidal rule and Simpson's rule are among the most common techniques for numerical integration. To approximate $\int_a^b f(x)\, dx$ let n be a positive integer and partition the interval $a \leqslant x \leqslant b$ into n equal subintervals of width $h = (b - a)/n$. Thus,

$$a = x_0 < x_1 < x_2 < \cdots < x_{n-1} < x_n = b$$

where

$$x_0 = a,\ x_1 = a + h,\ x_2 = a + 2h,\ \ldots,\ x_n = a + nh = b$$

Then the *trapezoidal rule* is

$$\int_a^b f(x)\, dx \approx [f(x_0) + f(x_1)]\frac{h}{2} + [f(x_1) + f(x_2)]\frac{h}{2}$$

$$+ \cdots + [f(x_{n-1}) + f(x_n)]\frac{h}{2}$$

and *Simpson's rule* is

$$\int_a^b f(x)\, dx \approx [f(x_0) + 4f(y_1) + f(x_1)]\frac{h}{6}$$

$$+ [f(x_1) + 4f(y_2) + f(x_2)]\frac{h}{6} + \cdots + [f(x_{n-1}) + 4f(y_n) + f(x_n)]\frac{h}{6}$$

where $y_i = 0.5(x_{i-1} + x_i)$ is the midpoint of the interval $x_{i-1} \leqslant x \leqslant x_i$.

If $f(x) \geqslant 0$, then $\int_a^b f(x)\, dx$ can be interpreted as the area under the graph of $y = f(x)$ and above the x-axis. The trapezoidal rule approximates the area using trapezoids, while Simpson's rule uses parabolas [11, 55] (see Figure 8-1). Generally, Simpson's rule gives a better approximation. As presented here, the trapezoidal rule uses n subintervals and Simpson's rule uses $2n$ subintervals.

The spreadsheet (Figure 8-2) uses $f(x) = x^2$, $n = 10$, $[a, b] = [0, 1]$. The trapezoidal-rule estimate is 0.335, while Simpson's rule shows 0.3333. (The true value of the integral is $1/3$. Simpson's rule gives exact answers for quadratic functions.) Note that the spreadsheet has been designed to allow up to $n = 100$ subintervals, that is, 200 for Simpson's rule. A different spreadsheet design which allows for more iterations is suggested in Exercise 33-6.

SPREADSHEET CONSTRUCTION

1. Enter the values for a and b into cells C5 and E5, the number of subintervals n into cell C6, (E5−C5)/C6, and the expression for determining h, into cell E6. Copy the values of a and b into cells B112 and C112.

2. Use column A as a counter, as indicated.

3. Enter the left endpoints of the first two subintervals, x_0 (+C5) and $x_0 + h$ (+B10+E6), into cells B10 and B11; enter the expression (E6/2+B10) for the first midpoint $h/2 + x_0$ into cell C10; and enter (+B10+E6), the first right endpoint $x_0 + h$, into cell D10. Create subsequent subintervals by replication in columns B, C, and D.

4. Compute the approximations of the area for the first subinterval:

   a. Trapezoidal: $[f(x_0) + f(x_1)](h/2)$; enter

   $$((B10*B10) + (D10*D10))*E6/2$$

   into cell E10.

   b. Simpson's: $[f(x_0) + 4f(y_1) + f(x_1)](h/6)$; enter

   $$((B10*B10) + (4*C10*C10) + (D10*D10))*E6/6$$

   into cell F10.

5. To find approximations for subsequent subintervals replicate the expressions in cells E10 and F10 (columns E and F).

6. Add the approximations from all subintervals. Enter

   @SUM(E10 . . . E109)   and   @SUM(F10 . . . F109)

   into cells E112 and F112. Note that rows 20 to 109 are blank, leaving room for later expansion to $n = 100$ subintervals.

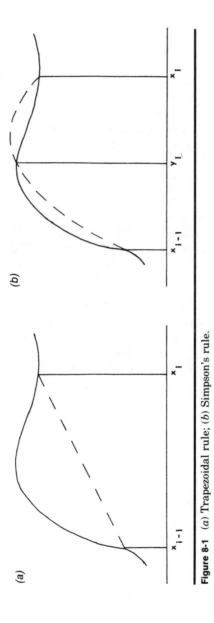

Figure 8-1 (a) Trapezoidal rule; (b) Simpson's rule.

Output

```
            A        B        C        D        E        F
        |-------|-------|-------|-------|-------|-------|-
    1             NUMERICAL    INTEGRATION
    2
    3       FROM A TO B IN N STEPS.   F(X) = X^2
    4
    5                    A=        0     B=        1
    6                    N=       10     H:       .1
    7
    8       COUNT    LEFT     MID    RIGHT     TRAP     SIMP
    9
   10         1       0      .05      .1     .0005    3.E-4
   11         2      .1      .15      .2     .0025    .0023
   12         3      .2      .25      .3     .0065    .0063
    :
   19        10      .9      .95     1.0     .0905    .0903
   20
    :
  110
  111      INTG.    FROM      TO               TRAP     SIMP
  112                0        1               .3350    .3333
```

Formulas (R)

```
         A          B             C            D            E            F
     |-------|---------|-------------|---------|-----------|---------|-
   5             A=        0              B=        1
   6             N=       10              H:      (E5-C5)/C6
   7
   8   COUNT    LEFT      MID          RIGHT     TRAP         SIMP
   9
  10   1        +C5       +E6/2+B10    +B10+E6   <E10>        <F10>
  11   1+A10    +B10+E6   +E6/2+B11    +B11+E6   <E11>        <F11>
  12   |1+A11   |+B11+E6  |+E6/2+B12   |+B12+E6  |<E12>       |<F12>
   :   Rep.     Rep.      Replicate    Rep.      Rep.         Rep.
   :   |[R]     |[RN]     |[NR]        |[RN]     |[RRRRN]     |[RRRRRRN]
  19   ↓1+A18   ↓+B18+E6  ↓+E6/2+B19   ↓+B19+E6  ↓<E19>       ↓<F19>
  20
   :
 110
 111   INTG.    FROM      TO                     TRAP         SIMP
 112            +C5       +E5                    <E112>       <F112>
```

Rows 20-110 are blank.

```
E10:  ((B10*B10)+(D10*D10))*E6/2
E11:  ((B11*B11)+(D11*D11))*E6/2
  :
E19:  ((B19*B19)+(D19*D19))*E6/2

F10:  ((B10*B10)+(4*C10*C10)+(D10*D10))*E6/6
F11:  ((B11*B11)+(4*C11*C11)+(D11*D11))*E6/6
  :
F19:  ((B19*B19)+(4*C19*C19)+(D19*D19))*E6/6

E112: @SUM(E10...E109)    F112: @SUM(F10...F109)
```

Figure 8-2 Numerical integration by the trapezoidal rule and Simpson's rule for $f(x) = x^2$.

USER INTERACTION

1. Change the endpoints a, b (cells C5 and E5).
2. Increase the number of subintervals n (cell C6) and replicate the expressions in row 19 appropriately.
3. Change the function by modifying the expressions in cells E10 and F10 and replicating (columns E and F). For example, if $f(x) = \sin x$, the expression in cell E10 is (@SIN(B10)+@SIN(D10))*E6/2.

Exercises and Modifications

8-1. Evaluate the following integrals:

a. $\int_1^4 \exp x \ dx$ b. $\int_0^1 \sin x \ dx$ c. $\int_1^2 \frac{1}{x} \ dx$

8-2. Experiment with various values of n for the same integral by modifying the spreadsheet (see also Exercise 33-6).

8-3. There are many other numerical integration algorithms [11]. Create a spreadsheet to implement some of them. For example, use Simpson's 3/8 rule:

$$\int_a^b f(x) \ dx \approx 3/8 \ [f(x_0) + 3f(y_1) + 3f(z_1) + f(x_1)] \frac{h}{3}$$

$$+ \ 3/8 \ [f(x_1) + 3f(y_2) + 3f(z_2) + f(x_2)] \frac{h}{3}$$

$$+ \cdots \cdots \cdots \cdots \cdots \cdots \cdots \cdots \cdots \cdots \cdots$$

$$+ \ 3/8 \ [f(x_{n-1}) + 3f(y_n) + 3f(z_n) + f(x_n)] \frac{h}{3}$$

where

$$y_i = x_{i-1} + \frac{h}{3} \qquad z_i = x_{i-1} + \frac{2h}{3} \qquad x_i = x_{i-1} + h$$

8-4. Modify the spreadsheet of this section so that a user can vary n ($1 \leq n \leq 100$) without having to adjust the rest of the spreadsheet. Change the expressions in cells E10 and F10 to

$$@IF(A10 > C6, 0, \text{———})$$

where the blank is the current entry in each of those cells. Replicate appropriate expressions in the spreadsheet through row 109. The values of entries in columns E and F will be 0 for iterations

$i > n$, and the approximating sums will appear in row 112. Use a horizontal window to improve the screen display.

REFERENCES

Trapezoidal and Simpson's rules: references 2, 5, 11, 22, 23, 30, 43, and 55.

Additional numerical integration: references 5, 11, 23, 30, and 59.

Demonstration

Taylor Polynomials

The nth-degree Taylor polynomial for a function $y = f(x)$ expanded about $x = a$ is given by

$$f(a) + f'(a)\frac{x - a}{1!} + f''(a)\frac{(x - a)^2}{2!} + \cdots + f^{(n)}(a)\frac{(x - a)^n}{n!}$$

This polynomial often provides a good approximation of $f(x)$ for x near a. The spreadsheet in Figure 9-1 is designed to evaluate Taylor polynomials expanded about $x = 0$:

$$P_n(x) = c_0 + c_1x + c_2x^2 + \cdots + c_nx^n$$

where

$$c_0 = f(0), \quad c_1 = \frac{f'(0)}{1!}, \quad c_2 = \frac{f''(0)}{2!}, \quad \cdots, \quad c_n = \frac{f^{(n)}(0)}{n!}$$

To use the spreadsheet, calculus must be employed to first determine the c_i. For example, if $f(x) = \exp x$, then

$$P_n(x) = 1 + \frac{1}{1!}x + \frac{1}{2!}x^2 + \cdots + \frac{1}{n!}x^n$$

Therefore

$$c_0 = 1, \quad c_1 = \frac{1}{1!}, \quad \cdots, \quad c_i = \frac{1}{i!}, \quad \cdots$$

and the c_i satisfy the recurrence relation

$$c_0 = 1 \qquad c_{i+1} = \frac{c_i}{i + 1} \qquad \text{for } i \geqslant 0$$

This recurrence relation can be used with replication to enter the c_i into the spreadsheet.

The spreadsheet (Figure 9-1) uses $f(x) = \exp x$ with $x = 2$ and displays the c_i, x^i, and ith terms of the expansion and the sum of the first i terms, for $i = 0, 1, 2, \ldots, n$. See how the values in the last column provide increasingly better approximations of $f(x)$. In this case, $\exp 2 \approx 7.3891$.

SPREADSHEET CONSTRUCTION

1. Enter the value of x into cell B3.

2. Use column A as a counter, as shown.

3. Enter the c_i into column B by means of a recurrence relation if possible. In this example enter $c_0 = 1$ into cell B6. Since $c_{i+1} = c_i/(i + 1)$, other terms in the sequence are found by dividing the

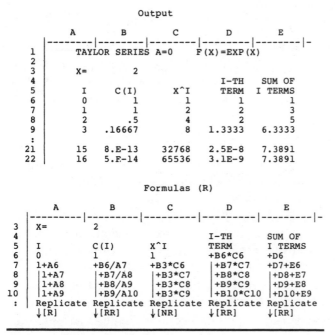

Output

	A	B	C	D	E
1		TAYLOR SERIES A=0		F(X)=EXP(X)	
2					
3	X=	2			
4				I-TH	SUM OF
5	I	C(I)	X^I	TERM	I TERMS
6	0	1	1	1	1
7	1	1	2	2	3
8	2	.5	4	2	5
9	3	.16667	8	1.3333	6.3333
:					
21	15	8.E-13	32768	2.5E-8	7.3891
22	16	5.F-14	65536	3.1E-9	7.3891

Formulas (R)

	A	B	C	D	E
3	X=	2			
4				I-TH	SUM OF
5	I	C(I)	X^I	TERM	I TERMS
6	0	1	1	+B6*C6	+D6
7	1+A6	+B6/A7	+B3*C6	+B7*C7	+D7+E6
8	1+A7	+B7/A8	+B3*C7	+B8*C8	+D8+E7
9	1+A8	+B8/A9	+B3*C8	+B9*C9	+D9+E8
10	1+A9	+B9/A10	+B3*C9	+B10*C10	+D10+E9
:	Replicate ↓[R]	Replicate ↓[RR]	Replicate ↓[NR]	Replicate ↓[RR]	Replicate ↓[RR]

Figure 9-1 Taylor polynomials.

previous term (cell above) by the current counter (cell to left). Enter +B6/A7 into cell B7 and replicate (column B).

4. Compute x^i in column C. Since $x^0 = 1$, enter 1 into cell C6. Compute successive powers of x by multiplying x times the previous power of x; enter +B3*C6 into cell C7 and replicate the expression down column C, with B3 (x) constant and C6 (the previous power of x) relative.

5. Calculate $c_i x^i$, the ith terms, in column D. Enter +B6*C6 into cell D6 and replicate (column D).

6. Calculate the sum of the first i terms in column E. Enter the first term, +D6, into cell E6. In general, the ith sum is the ith term (cell to the left) plus the $(i - 1)$th sum (cell above). Enter +D7+E6 into cell E7 and replicate (column E).

USER INTERACTION

1. Evaluate the Taylor polynomial for various values of x (cell B3).

2. Enter the coefficients for the Taylor polynomial of another function (cells B6, B7, B8, . . .).

3. Obtain more terms of the Taylor polynomial by replicating the expressions in the final row.

Exercises and Modifications

9-1. Enter the coefficients for the Taylor polynomial for the cosine expanded about $x = 0$. Note that the coefficients, 1, 0, $-1/2!$, 0, $1/4!$, 0, $-1/6!$, . . . , can be described by the recurrence relation

$$c_0 = 1, \ c_1 = 0, \ c_i = \frac{-c_{i-2}}{(i - 1)i} \qquad i > 1$$

Evaluate $\cos x$ at $x = 0$, $\pi/4$, $\pi/2$, π, $3\pi/2$, 2π, . . . and observe that more terms are needed to obtain a good approximation as the distance from 0 to x increases.

9-2. Enter the coefficients for the Taylor expansions of $\sin x$, $\ln (1 + x)$, $1/(1 - x)$, $1/(1 + x)$, $\tan x$, and $\sqrt{1 + x}$ expanded about $x = 0$; find recurrence relations for the c_i. Investigate the convergence of the resulting approximation by varying the value of x (cell B3).

9-3. Create a spreadsheet to find polynomial expansions of $f(x)$ about an arbitrary point $x = a$, where a is a parameter.

9-4. Modify the spreadsheet to include a column that estimates $f'(x)$ as well as $f(x)$.

9-5. There are various estimates for the error that arises in approximating a function by a Taylor polynomial. Modify the spreadsheet
to include a column which estimates the error.[55, p. 534].

REFERENCES

Taylor series and Taylor polynomials: references 2, 11, 22, 30, 43, and 55.

Demonstration

Differential Equations
Euler's Method

Euler's method is the most elementary of the numerical algorithms for approximating a solution to an initial-value problem (IVP)

$$y' = f(x, y) \qquad y(x_0) = y_0$$

To use Euler's method in estimating the solution on the interval $x \geqslant x_0$, choose a step size $h > 0$. Define x_i by

$$x_1 = x_0 + h, \, x_2 = x_0 + 2h, \, \ldots, \, x_n = x_0 + nh$$

Then

$$x_{i+1} = x_i + h \qquad \text{for } i \geqslant 0$$

Set $Y_0 = y_0$. If Y_i denotes the approximation of $y(x_i)$,

$$Y_{i+1} = Y_i + hf(x_i, Y_i) \qquad i \geqslant 0$$

Euler's algorithm is illustrated in Figure 10-1.

Euler's algorithm provides an easily derived approximation to the solution of an IVP. Unfortunately, the approximation is usually rather inexact. Although decreasing h may improve the approximation, it creates other difficulties [5, p. 308; 11 p. 189]. More sophisticated numerical methods for solving IVPs are given by the Heun algorithm, the improved Euler algorithm, and various Runge-Kutta algorithms, each of which can be set up in a spreadsheet using a format similar to that of the Euler algorithm.

The spreadsheet in Figure 10-2 illustrates Euler's method using $f(x, y) = x + y$ with $h = 0.01$. Values for x_0, y_0, and h are entered by the user. A modification of this spreadsheet appears in Figure 33-4.

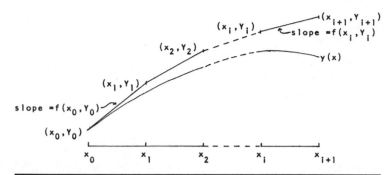

Figure 10-1   Euler's algorithm.

SPREADSHEET CONSTRUCTION

1. Enter x_0 and y_0, the initial values of x and y, into cells B4 and B5 and the value of h into cell B6.

2. Copy x_0 (+B4) into cell A9 and y_0 (+B5) into cell B9.

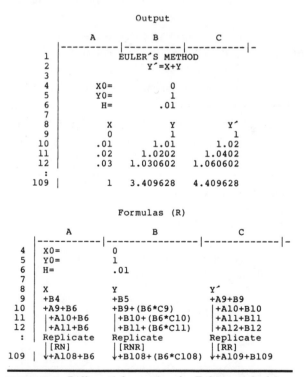

```
                           Output

                  A          B          C
            |----------|----------|----------|-
      1              EULER'S METHOD
      2                 Y'=X+Y
      3
      4         X0=         0
      5         Y0=         1
      6         H=         .01
      7
      8         X          Y          Y'
      9         0          1          1
     10        .01        1.01       1.02
     11        .02       1.0202     1.0402
     12        .03      1.030602   1.060602
      :
    109 |       1        3.409628   4.409628
```

```
                       Formulas (R)

              A                   B                   C
       |------------|-------------------|----------------|-
   4   X0=          0
   5   Y0=          1
   6   H=          .01
   7
   8   X            Y                   Y'
   9   +B4          +B5                 +A9+B9
  10   +A9+B6       +B9+(B6*C9)         +A10+B10
  11   |+A10+B6     |+B10+(B6*C10)      |+A11+B11
  12   |+A11+B6     |+B11+(B6*C11)      |+A12+B12
   :   |Replicate   Replicate           Replicate
       |[RN]        |[RNR]              |[RR]
 109 | ↓+A108+B6   ↓+B108+(B6*C108)    ↓+A109+B109
```

Figure 10-2   Differential equations by Euler's method for $y' = x + y$, $y(0) = 1$.

3. Columns A, B, and C contain the values of x_i, Y_i, and $f(x_i, Y_i)$, respectively. Since $f(x + y) = x + y$, enter +A9+B9 into cell C9 to find $f(x_0, Y_0)$. In the next iteration $x_1 = x_0 + h$; enter +A9+B6 into cell A10. Also, $Y_1 = Y_0 + hf(x_0, Y_0)$; enter +B9+(B6*C9) into cell B10.

4. To carry out additional iterations, replicate the expressions in cells A10, B10, and C9 (columns A, B, and C).

USER INTERACTION

1. Change h (cell B6); change initial values x_0 and y_0 (cells B4 and B5).

2. Change the differential equation by changing the expression for $f(x, y)$ in cell C9 and replicating (column C).

Exercises and Modifications

10-1. Use $h = 0.005$ in the example and extend the spreadsheet to twice its original length; use $h = 0.1$ and cause only 10 iterations to be shown.

10-2. Solve the IVP $y' = x + y$, $y(0) = 1$ analytically and add a column to the spreadsheet to compare that solution with the Euler approximation at $x = 0, 0.01, 0.02, 0.03, \ldots$.

10-3. Create a spreadsheet to obtain a numerical approximation to the solution of the IVP $y' = 3y + x$, $y(1) = 2$.

10-4. Create a spreadsheet to implement another numerical IVP algorithm, e.g., improved Euler, Heun, or Runge-Kutta [11, 65]. Combine two or more algorithms on the same spreadsheet.

10-5. Extend Euler's method to higher-order differential equations and construct the appropriate spreadsheets.

REFERENCES

Numerical solutions of IVPs: references 5, 11, 22, 23, 30, 61, and 65.

Polynomial Interpolation:
Neville's Algorithm

Suppose that f is a continuous function on an interval $[a, b]$ and that $f(a)$ and $f(b)$ are known. Linear interpolation [11, 22] (Figure 11-1a) can be used to estimate the value of $f(c)$, $a \leq c \leq b$, by approximating $y = f(x)$ on the interval $[a, b]$ with the straight line through the points $(a, f(a))$ and $(b, f(b))$

$$\frac{y - f(a)}{x - a} = \frac{f(b) - f(a)}{b - a}$$

so that

$$f(c) \approx f(a) + (c - a)\frac{f(b) - f(a)}{b - a}$$

This process can be generalized if f is known at $n + 1$ points

$$(x_0, y_0), (x_1, y_1), \ldots, (x_n, y_n)$$

where

$$a = x_0 < x_1 < \cdots < x_{n-1} < x_n = b$$

It is always possible to find a polynomial of degree at most n which passes through these points. It is called the *Lagrange interpolating polynomial* $p_n(x)$ [11, p. 82]; $p_n(x)$ can be used to estimate (interpolate) the value of $f(c)$ at a point $x = c$ between a and b (see Figure 11-1b). Neville's algorithm [11, 28] is a method for evaluating $p_n(c)$. The recursive description of the algorithm is listed below. For $n = 1$, the algorithm results in linear interpolation.

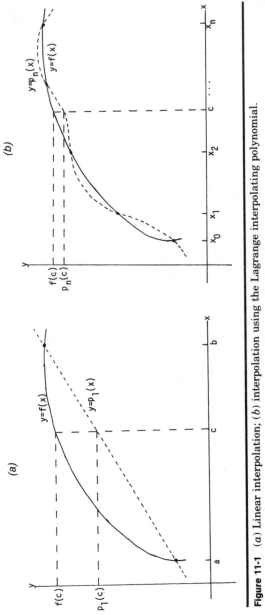

Figure 11-1 (*a*) Linear interpolation; (*b*) interpolation using the Lagrange interpolating polynomial.

Set $P_{0,0}(x) = y_0, P_{1,0}(x) = y_1, \ldots, P_{n,0}(x) = y_n$, and for $i \geqslant j$ let $P_{i,j}(x)$ be the polynomial of degree at most $j > 0$ passing through the $j + 1$ points $(x_{i-j}, y_{i-j}), \ldots, (x_i, y_i)$. Then

$$P_{i,j}(x) = \frac{(x - x_{i-j})P_{i,j-1}(x) - (x - x_i)P_{i-1,j-1}(x)}{x_i - x_{i-j}}$$

and

$$f(c) \approx p_n(c) = P_{n,n}(c)$$

The algorithm is carried out in table format:

x_0	$P_{0,0}$				
x_1	$P_{1,0}$	$P_{1,1}$			
x_2	$P_{2,0}$	$P_{2,1}$	$P_{2,2}$		
. . .	. . . . .	. . . .	. . . .	. . . .	. . .
x_{n-1}	$P_{n-1,0}$	$P_{n-1,1}$	$P_{n-1,2}$ $\cdots$	$P_{n-1,n-1}$	
x_n	$P_{n,0}$	$P_{n,1}$	$P_{n,2}$ $\cdots$	$P_{n,n-1}$	$P_{n,n}$

The spreadsheet in Figure 11-2 implements Neville's algorithm using $n = 4$. If f is given by the indicated data, $f(1.6) \approx 0.6901$.

We introduce here a space-saving notation used to refer to a rectangular block of cells in the spreadsheet. The sign $\|$ signals the beginning and end of this notation, in which the first cell represents the upper left-hand cell of the block and the second represents the lower right-hand cell of the block. Thus the notation $\|$A6 to B10$\|$ is shorthand for cells A6 to A10 and B6 to B10. Similarly $\|$D3 to G5$\|$ stands for D3 to D5, E3 to E5, . . . , G3 to G5.

SPREADSHEET CONSTRUCTION

1. Enter the x and y coordinates into cells $\|$A6 to B10$\|$ and the value of c into cell A3; copy the latter into cell F12.
2. The recurrence relation gives the top entry of column i by

$$P_{i,i} = \frac{(c - x_0)P_{i,i-1} - (c - x_i)P_{i-1,i-1}}{x_i - x_0}$$

Enter

$$(((A3-A6)*B7)-((A3-A7)*B6))/(A7-A6)$$

into cell C7,

$$(((A3-A6)*C8)-((A3-A8)*C7))/(A8-A6)$$

into cell D8, and so forth. The expressions for other cells can be generated by replicating these expressions appropriately down columns.

USER INTERACTION

1. Vary the value of c (cell A3).
2. Change the x and y values of the given data in cells ‖A6 to B10‖.

Exercises and Modifications

11-1. Enter 1.2, 1.5, 1.8, 2.1, 2.4 for c and observe that the algorithm agrees with the corresponding given values of y.

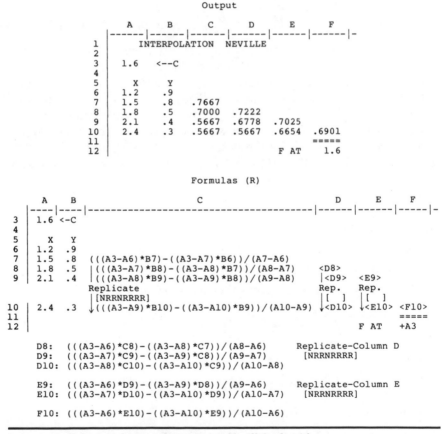

```
                                Output

                A      B      C      D      E      F
             |------|------|------|------|------|------|-
          1  |      INTERPOLATION   NEVILLE
          2  |
          3  | 1.6    <--C
          4  |
          5  |   X      Y
          6  | 1.2     .9
          7  | 1.5     .8    .7667
          8  | 1.8     .5    .7000  .7222
          9  | 2.1     .4    .5667  .6778  .7025
         10  | 2.4     .3    .5667  .5667  .6654  .6901
         11  |                                    =====
         12  |                             F AT   1.6


                             Formulas (R)

       A    B                        C                         D      E      F
    |----|----|-----------------------------------------------|------|------|-----|-
  3 | 1.6 <-C
  4 |
  5 |  X    Y
  6 | 1.2  .9
  7 | 1.5  .8  (((A3-A6)*B7)-((A3-A7)*B6))/(A7-A6)
  8 | 1.8  .5 |(((A3-A7)*B8)-((A3-A8)*B7))/(A8-A7)    <D8>
  9 | 2.1  .4 |(((A3-A8)*B9)-((A3-A9)*B8))/(A9-A8)    |<D9>   <E9>
    |         Replicate                               Rep.   Rep.
    |         |[NRRNRRRR]                            |[  ]  |[  ]
 10 | 2.4  .3 ↓(((A3-A9)*B10)-((A3-A10)*B9))/(A10-A9) ↓<D10> ↓<E10> <F10>
 11 |                                                               =====
 12 |                                                        F AT   +A3


       D8:  (((A3-A6)*C8)-((A3-A8)*C7))/(A8-A6)    Replicate-Column D
       D9:  (((A3-A7)*C9)-((A3-A9)*C8))/(A9-A7)       [NRRNRRRR]
       D10: (((A3-A8)*C10)-((A3-A10)*C9))/(A10-A8)

       E9:  (((A3-A6)*D9)-((A3-A9)*D8))/(A9-A6)    Replicate-Column E
       E10: (((A3-A7)*D10)-((A3-A10)*D9))/(A10-A7)    [NRRNRRRR]

       F10: (((A3-A6)*E10)-((A3-A10)*E9))/(A10-A6)
```

Figure 11-2   Polynomial interpolation using Neville's algorithm.

11-2. Use interpolation with the following data to estimate $f(x)$ for $x = 1.2$, 3.3, and 3.4:

x	0	1	2	3	4
$f(x)$	3	7	9	10	12

11-3. Create a spreadsheet for Neville's algorithm using $n + 1$ points for values of n other than $n = 4$. Note that $n = 1$ gives linear interpolation.

11-4. Consult a book on numerical analysis for other interpolation schemes and create spreadsheet implementations. For example, Aitken's method [28] uses the recurrence relation

$$Q_{i,j} = \frac{(x - x_i)Q_{j-1,j-1} - (x - x_{j-1})Q_{i,j-1}}{x_{j-1} - x_i}$$

REFERENCES

Interpolation: references 5, 11, 23, 28, 30, and 59.

Neville's and Aitken's algorithms: references 11 and 28.

Linear interpolation: references 11, 19, 33, and 34.

Matrix Multiplication

Matrix multiplication is defined for two 3×3 matrices by

$$\begin{bmatrix} a_{11} & a_{12} & a_{13} \\ a_{21} & a_{22} & a_{23} \\ a_{31} & a_{32} & a_{33} \end{bmatrix} \begin{bmatrix} b_{11} & b_{12} & b_{13} \\ b_{21} & b_{22} & b_{23} \\ b_{31} & b_{32} & b_{33} \end{bmatrix} = \begin{bmatrix} c_{11} & c_{12} & c_{13} \\ c_{21} & c_{22} & c_{23} \\ c_{31} & c_{32} & c_{33} \end{bmatrix}$$

where

$$c_{ij} = a_{i1}b_{1j} + a_{i2}b_{2j} + a_{i3}b_{3j}$$

In general, if $A = [a_{ij}]$ is an $n \times p$ matrix and $B = [b_{ij}]$ is a $p \times m$ matrix, then $C = AB = [c_{ij}]$ is the $n \times m$ matrix defined by

$$c_{ij} = a_{i1}b_{1j} + a_{i2}b_{2j} + \cdots + a_{ip}b_{pj}$$

The last expression is called the *dot product* of row i of A and column j of B.

Matrix multiplication is easy to implement using a spreadsheet. The formula for only one entry of the product need be entered directly; the rest can be entered by replication. The spreadsheet (Figure 12-1) finds the product of two 3×3 matrices. The construction for matrices of other dimensions is similar.

SPREADSHEET CONSTRUCTION

1. Enter matrix A into cells ‖A5 to C7‖ and matrix B into cells ‖E5 to G7‖.

2. Enter the formula for the dot product of row 1 of matrix A and column 1 of matrix B

$$(A5*E5)+(B5*E6)+(C5*E7)$$

into cell A10.

3. Replicate the expression in cell A10 across row 10, treating A5, B5, and C5 (the variables of the first row of matrix A) as constant locations and E5, E6, and E7 (the column variables of matrix B) as relative locations.

4. Replicate the expressions in row 10 into rows 11 and 12, treating the first, third, and fifth variables (the row variables of matrix A) as relative locations and the second, fourth, and sixth variables (the column variables of matrix B) as constant locations.

USER INTERACTION

Vary the matrices A and B in cells ‖A5 to C7‖ and ‖E5 to G7‖.

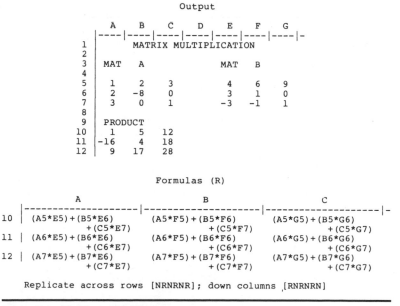

Figure 12-1 Matrix multiplication.

Exercises and Modifications

12-1. Find the product

$$\begin{bmatrix} 3 & 4 & 5 \\ 3 & 1 & 9 \\ 0 & 4 & 0 \end{bmatrix} \begin{bmatrix} 8 & 7 & -1 \\ 9 & -5 & 0 \\ 2 & 2 & 3 \end{bmatrix}$$

12-2. Modify the spreadsheet to find the product of $n \times p$ and $p \times m$ matrices for various n, p, and m.

12-3. Let either matrix A or B be an elementary matrix [64] and investigate the effect of the multiplication. For example, set

$$A = \begin{bmatrix} 1 & 0 & 0 \\ 0 & 3 & 0 \\ 0 & 0 & 1 \end{bmatrix}$$

and observe that multiplying B on the left by A, that is, finding the product AB, multiplies the second row of B by 3.

12-4. Create a spreadsheet to multiply three matrices of appropriate dimensions. Calculate the answer two ways and verify the associative property

$$(AB)C = A(BC)$$

REFERENCES

Matrix multiplication: references 1, 10, 18, 35, 36, 40, 48, 53, 63, and 64.

Matrix multiplication applications: references 1, 10, 35, 46, 50, 63, and 64.

Elementary matrices: references 35 and 64.

Jacobi and Gauss-Seidel Algorithms

The solution of a linear system of equations of the form

$$
\begin{aligned}
x_1 &= \phantom{b_{21}x_1} b_{12}x_2 + b_{13}x_3 + c_1 \\
x_2 &= b_{21}x_1 \phantom{+ b_{12}x_2} + b_{23}x_3 + c_2 \\
x_3 &= b_{31}x_1 + b_{32}x_2 \phantom{+ b_{23}x_3} + c_3
\end{aligned}
$$

can often be found using the Jacobi and the Gauss-Seidel iterative algorithms.

Let $x_1^{(0)}$, $x_2^{(0)}$, and $x_3^{(0)}$ be an initial estimate of the solution. The $(n + 1)$th approximation is obtained from the nth approximation by the Jacobi algorithm

$$
\begin{aligned}
x_1^{(n+1)} &= \phantom{b_{21}x_1^{(n)}} b_{12}x_2^{(n)} + b_{13}x_3^{(n)} + c_1 \\
x_2^{(n+1)} &= b_{21}x_1^{(n)} \phantom{+ b_{12}x_2^{(n)}} + b_{23}x_3^{(n)} + c_2 \\
x_3^{(n+1)} &= b_{31}x_1^{(n)} + b_{32}x_2^{(n)} \phantom{+ b_{23}x_3^{(n)}} + c_3
\end{aligned}
$$

or the Gauss-Seidel algorithm

$$
\begin{aligned}
x_1^{(n+1)} &= \phantom{b_{21}x_1^{(n+1)}} b_{12}x_2^{(n)} + b_{13}x_3^{(n)} + c_1 \\
x_2^{(n+1)} &= b_{21}x_1^{(n+1)} \phantom{+ b_{12}x_2^{(n)}} + b_{23}x_3^{(n)} + c_2 \\
x_3^{(n+1)} &= b_{31}x_1^{(n+1)} + b_{32}x_2^{(n+1)} \phantom{+ b_{23}x_3^{(n)}} + c_3
\end{aligned}
$$

The Jacobi algorithm uses nth-step estimates in all computations at step $n + 1$. The Gauss-Seidel algorithm incorporates the $(n + 1)$th-step estimates in the computations at step $n + 1$ as soon as they become available. Generally, but not always, the Gauss-Seidel algorithm converges faster than the Jacobi algorithm. Sometimes one converges but not the other (Exercise 13-4) or neither converges (Exercise 13-3). Convergence is discussed in Refs. 11 and 59.

The spreadsheet (Figures 13-1 and 13-2) converges for any initial estimate using either algorithm. The solution of the given system is $(x_1, x_2, x_3) = (1, 4, -2)$.

SPREADSHEET CONSTRUCTION

1. Enter the matrix of the system into cells ‖B4 to E6‖; enter the initial estimate $x_1^{(0)}$, $x_2^{(0)}$, $x_3^{(0)}$ into cells B9, C9, and D9.

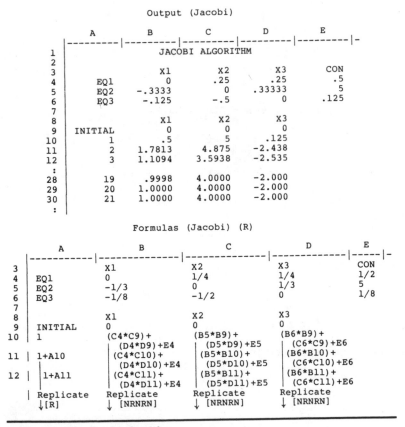

Output (Jacobi)

	A	B	C	D	E
1			JACOBI ALGORITHM		
2					
3			X1	X2	X3	CON
4	EQ1	0	.25	.25	.5
5	EQ2	-.3333	0	.33333	5
6	EQ3	-.125	-.5	0	.125
7					
8			X1	X2	X3	
9	INITIAL	0	0	0	
10	1	.5	5	.125	
11	2	1.7813	4.875	-2.438	
12	3	1.1094	3.5938	-2.535	
:					
28	19	.9998	4.0000	-2.000	
29	20	1.0000	4.0000	-2.000	
30	21	1.0000	4.0000	-2.000	
:					

Formulas (Jacobi) (R)

	A	B	C	D	E
3		X1	X2	X3	CON
4	EQ1	0	1/4	1/4	1/2
5	EQ2	-1/3	0	1/3	5
6	EQ3	-1/8	-1/2	0	1/8
7					
8		X1	X2	X3	
9	INITIAL	0	0	0	
10	1	(C4*C9)+(D4*D9)+E4	(B5*B9)+(D5*D9)+E5	(B6*B9)+(C6*C9)+E6	
11	1+A10	(C4*C10)+(D4*D10)+E4	(B5*B10)+(D5*D10)+E5	(B6*B10)+(C6*C10)+E6	
12	1+A11	(C4*C11)+(D4*D11)+E4	(B5*B11)+(D5*D11)+E5	(B6*B11)+(C6*C11)+E6	
	Replicate ↓[R]	Replicate ↓ [NRNRN]	Replicate ↓ [NRNRN]	Replicate ↓ [NRNRN]	

Figure 13-1 The Jacobi algorithm.

$$x_1 = \qquad \tfrac{1}{4}x_2 + \tfrac{1}{4}x_3 + \tfrac{1}{2}$$
$$x_2 = -\tfrac{1}{3}x_1 \qquad\qquad + \tfrac{1}{3}x_3 + 5$$
$$x_3 = -\tfrac{1}{8}x_1 - \tfrac{1}{2}x_2 \qquad + \tfrac{1}{8}$$

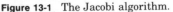

2. Since

$$x_1^{(1)} = b_{12}x_2^{(0)} + b_{13}x_3^{(0)} + c_1$$

enter

$$(C4*C9)+(D4*D9)+E4$$

into cell B10 and replicate (column B).

3. Enter the indicated Jacobi or Gauss-Seidel expressions for $x_2^{(1)}$ and $x_3^{(1)}$ into cells C10 and D10 and replicate (columns C and D). Note that the Jacobi algorithm (Figure 13-1) always uses values from the previous row. The Gauss-Seidel algorithm (Figure 13-2) uses values from the current row as they become available.

4. Use column A as a counter.

USER INTERACTION

1. Change initial estimates for the roots (cells B9, C9, and D9).

2. Change the equation coefficients and constants to solve other systems (cells ∥B4 to E6∥).

Exercises and Modifications

13-1. Change the initial estimate to:
   a. $(4, 3, 2)$ b. $(1, 4, -2)$ c. $(1, 3, -1)$

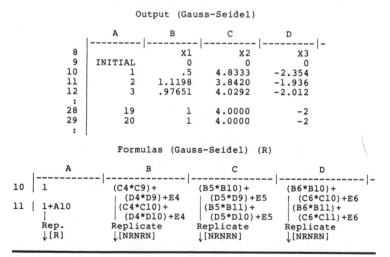

```
                    Output (Gauss-Seidel)

                 A          B          C          D
        --------- |--------- |--------- |--------- |-
    8                        X1         X2         X3
    9    INITIAL   0          0          0
   10       1      .5        4.8333    -2.354
   11       2     1.1198     3.8420    -1.936
   12       3      .97651    4.0292    -2.012
    :
   28      19      1         4.0000     -2
   29      20      1         4.0000     -2
    :
```

```
                    Formulas (Gauss-Seidel)  (R)

             A                B               C               D
      |------------- |--------------- |--------------- |--------------- |-
  10  | 1            (C4*C9)+          (B5*B10)+         (B6*B10)+
      |              (D4*D9)+E4        (D5*D9)+E5        (C6*C10)+E6
  11  | 1+A10        (C4*C10)+         (B5*B11)+         (B6*B11)+
      |              (D4*D10)+E4       (D5*D11)+E5       (C6*C11)+E6
      | Rep.         Replicate         Replicate         Replicate
      | ↓[R]         ↓[NRNRN]          ↓[NRNRN]          ↓[NRNRN]
```

Figure 13-2 The Gauss-Seidel algorithm.

13-2. Use either the Jacobi or the Gauss-Seidel algorithm to solve the system below. System (b) fits the format of the algorithms and is derived from system (a) by solving each of the equations for a different variable. It can be shown that both algorithms will converge for system (b) if the matrix of coefficients of system (a) is diagonally dominant [11, p. 389].

a. $3x_1 - x_2 + x_3 = -1$ b. $x_1 = \frac{1}{3}x_2 - \frac{1}{3}x_3 - \frac{1}{3}$
  $3x_1 + 9x_2 + 5x_3 = 4$ $x_2 = -\frac{3}{9}x_1 - \frac{5}{9}x_3 + \frac{4}{9}$
  $3x_1 + 3x_2 + 8x_3 = 0$ $x_3 = -\frac{3}{8}x_1 - \frac{3}{8}x_2$

13-3. Try the algorithms on the following system; notice that neither algorithm converges:

$$x_1 = \quad -1.5x_2 - 2x_3 + 4$$
$$x_2 = -x_1 \quad\quad - x_3 + 4$$
$$x_3 = -3x_1 + x_2 \quad\quad + 6$$

13-4. Try the algorithms on the following systems; notice that only one of the algorithms converges for each [60, p. 74]:

a. $x_1 = -2x_2 + 2x_3 + 1$ b. $x_1 = 0.5x_2 - 0.5x_3 + 1$
  $x_1 = -x_1 - x_3 + 2$ $x_2 = -x_1 - x_3 + 2$
  $x_3 = -2x_1 - 2x_1 + 3$ $x_3 = 0.5x_1 + 0.5x_2 + 3$

13-5. Enter both the Jacobi and Gauss-Seidel algorithms on the same spreadsheet. Compare the rates of convergence.

13-6. Modify the spreadsheets for use with 2×2, 4×4, 5×5, . . . systems.

REFERENCES

Gauss-Seidel and Jacobi algorithms: references 5, 11, 23, 30, 36, 59, 60, and 61.

Dominant Eigenvalue via Iteration
Power Method

If $A = [a_{ij}]$ is an $n \times n$ matrix, λ is an *eigenvalue* of A if there is a nonzero vector $\mathbf{v}$ for which $A\mathbf{v} = \lambda\mathbf{v}$. Any vector $\mathbf{v}$ satisfying this condition is called an *eigenvector* corresponding to λ (see also Demonstration 15). For example, $\lambda = 3$ is an eigenvalue of A, and $\mathbf{v}$ is a corresponding eigenvector, where

$$A = \begin{bmatrix} 0 & 2 \\ -3 & 5 \end{bmatrix} \quad \text{and} \quad \mathbf{v} = \begin{bmatrix} 2 \\ 3 \end{bmatrix}$$

since

$$\begin{bmatrix} 0 & 2 \\ -3 & 5 \end{bmatrix}\begin{bmatrix} 2 \\ 3 \end{bmatrix} = 3\begin{bmatrix} 2 \\ 3 \end{bmatrix}$$

Eigenvalues and eigenvectors appear throughout mathematics in such areas as geometry [64], differential equations [65], and Fibonacci numbers [1] and in applied areas such as genetics [46] and mechanics [26]. In a number of applications the eigenvalue having the largest absolute value (called the *dominant eigenvalue*) is the most important. This eigenvalue can often be found by iterative algorithms, one of which (the power method) is described below. (All vectors in this demonstration are column vectors; they have been written in lines of text as their transposed form, i.e., as row vectors, to condense notation.)

Let A be an $n \times n$ real matrix having n distinct eigenvalues: $\lambda_1, \lambda_2,$ . . . with $|\lambda_1| > |\lambda_j|$ for $j = 2, 3, \ldots, n$. Let $\mathbf{V} = [v_1^{(0)} \quad v_2^{(0)} \quad \cdots$ $v_n^{(0)}]^T$ be an initial vector, m_o the component of $\mathbf{V}_0$ of largest absolute value, and $\mathbf{W}_o = \mathbf{V}_o/m_o$. Define vectors $\mathbf{V}_i = [v_1^{(i)} \quad v_2^{(i)} \quad \cdots \quad v_n^{(i)}]^T$ and $\mathbf{W}_i$, for $i > 0$, recursively by

$$\mathbf{V}_i = A\mathbf{W}_{i-1} \qquad \mathbf{W}_i = \frac{\mathbf{V}_i}{m_i}$$

where m_i is the component of $\mathbf{V}_i$ having the largest absolute value. It can be shown that unless the original vector $\mathbf{V}_o$ is itself an eigenvector belonging to another eigenvalue, the sequence m_i converges to the dominant eigenvalue λ_1 of A and the vectors $\mathbf{W}_i$ converge to a corresponding eigenvector [5, p. 514].

The spreadsheet (Figure 14-1) employs this algorithm for 2×2 matrices. For ease of notation, set $x = v_1$, $y = v_2$. Note that the x and y

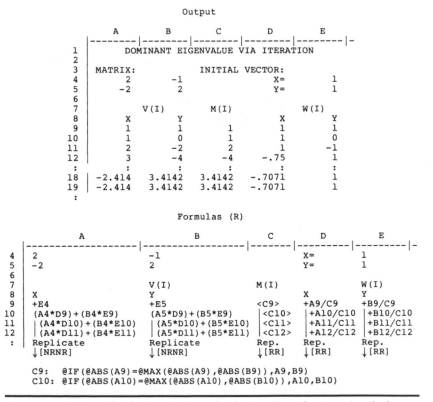

Figure 14-1   Finding the dominant eigenvalue by iteration: the power method.

components of **V** are in columns A and B, the m_i (the component of $\mathbf{V}_i$ having the larger absolute value) are in column C, and the x and y components of $\mathbf{W}_i$ ($\mathbf{V}_i$ divided by m_i) are in columns D and E. From the spreadsheet output in Figure 14-1 observe that the dominant eigenvalue of A is approximately 3.4142 and that a corresponding eigenvector is approximately $[-0.7071 \quad 1]^T$, where

$$A = \begin{bmatrix} a_{11} & a_{12} \\ a_{21} & a_{22} \end{bmatrix} = \begin{bmatrix} 2 & -1 \\ -2 & 2 \end{bmatrix}$$

SPREADSHEET CONSTRUCTION

1. Enter the matrix and initial vector into cells ‖A4 to B5‖ and E4 and E5. Copy the initial vector into cells A9 and B9 as $[x^{(0)} \quad y^{(0)}]$.

2. a. Cell C9 contains m_o, the value in A8 and B9 that is larger in absolute value: enter

   @IF@ABS(A9)=@MAX(@ABS(A9),@ABS(B9)),A9,B9)

   b. Cells D9 and E9 contain $\mathbf{W}_o = \mathbf{V}_o/m_o$. Enter +A9/C9 and +B9/C9.

   c. Cells A10 and B10 contain $\mathbf{V}_1 = [x^{(1)} \quad y^{(1)}]^T = A\mathbf{W}_o$. Since

   $$x^{(1)} = a_{11}W_x^{(0)} + a_{12}W_y^{(0)} \qquad \text{and} \qquad y^{(1)} = a_{21}W_x^{(0)} + a_{22}W_y^{(0)}$$

   enter (A4*D9)+(B4*E9) into cell A10 and (A5*D9)+(B5*E9) into cell B10.

3. Additional iterations are obtained by replicating expressions down columns as indicated.

USER INTERACTION

1. Change the initial vector cells (E4 and E5).
2. Change the matrix in cells ‖A4 to B5‖.

Exercises and Modifications

14-1. Enter another eigenvector, $[1 \quad \sqrt{2}]^T$, as the initial vector in cells E4 and E5. Observe what happens. Generate a large number of iterations. Compare the results with part (d) of 14-2.

14-2. For the following matrices, first find the eigenvalues by hand, noting their absolute values. Then use the spreadsheet algorithm and observe the rate of convergence. In part d use $[1 \quad 1]^T$ and then $[-1 \quad 1]^T$ as the initial vectors.

a. $\begin{bmatrix} 2 & -1 \\ 5 & 7 \end{bmatrix}$ b. $\begin{bmatrix} 9 & 1 \\ 0 & -1.9 \end{bmatrix}$ c. $\begin{bmatrix} 2 & 1 \\ 0 & -1.9 \end{bmatrix}$ d. $\begin{bmatrix} 2 & 3 \\ 1 & 0 \end{bmatrix}$

14-3. Design spreadsheets to implement the algorithm for 3×3 and larger matrices.

14-4. If A is an invertible matrix and λ is the dominant eigenvalue of A^{-1}, then $1/\lambda$ is the eigenvalue of A having the smallest absolute value. Modify the 2×2 spreadsheet to calculate A^{-1} and use it to find the smaller eigenvalue of A.

REFERENCES

Eigenvalues and eigenvectors: references 1, 24, 36, 46, 53, and 64.

Iterative algorithms for eigenvalues: references 1, 5, 11, 23, 24, 30, and 36.

Fibonacci sequence and matrices: references 1, 36, and 53.

Mechanics: reference 26.

15

Eigenvalues and Diagonalization

Recall from Demonstration 14 that a number λ is an eigenvalue of a square matrix A if there is a nonzero vector $\mathbf{v}$ satisfying $A\mathbf{v} = \lambda\mathbf{v}$. Any vector satisfying this equation is called an eigenvector corresponding to λ. The spreadsheet (Figure 15-1) determines real eigenvalues of a 2×2 matrix A and finds an invertible matrix P (if one exists) so that $P^{-1}AP$ is a diagonal matrix. Such a matrix P is said to *diagonalize* A. Applications of these concepts occur in geometry, systems of linear differential equations, and many other areas [1, 46, 64].

The results used in this demonstration are not hard to derive from a knowledge of linear algebra and are left to the reader. For a discussion of the concepts and the background needed, see Refs. 1 and 64. As before, we use the transpose of column vectors to conserve space.

An eigenvalue λ of

$$A = \begin{bmatrix} a & b \\ c & d \end{bmatrix}$$

satisfies

$$\det(A - \lambda I) = \begin{vmatrix} a - \lambda & b \\ c & d - \lambda \end{vmatrix} = \lambda^2 - (a + d)\lambda + (ad - bc) = 0$$

Therefore

$$\lambda = \frac{a + d \pm \sqrt{(a - d)^2 + 4bc}}{2}$$

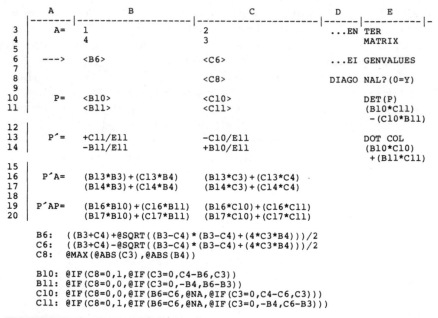

Output

```
          A         B         C         D         E
      |-------|-------|-------|-------|-------|-
   1       EIGENVALUES AND DIAGONALIZATION
   2
   3      A=        1         2      ...ENTER
   4                4         3          MATRIX
   5
   6   ---->     5.00     -1.00      ...EIGENVALUES
   7
   8                       4.00      DIAGONAL?(0=Y)
   9
  10      P=     2.00      2.00         DET(P)
  11             4.00     -2.00         -12
  12
  13      P'=    0.17      0.17         DOT COL
  14             0.33     -0.17         -4
  15
  16      P'A=   0.83      0.83
  17            -0.33      0.17
  18
  19     P'AP=   5.00      0.00
  20             0.00     -1.00
```

Formulas (R)

```
        A              B                      C                 D        E
   |-------|---------------------|-----------------------|------|----------|-
  3     A=   1                     2                        ...EN TER
  4          4                     3                              MATRIX
  5
  6   --->   <B6>                  <C6>                     ...EI GENVALUES
  7
  8                                <C8>                     DIAGO NAL?(0=Y)
  9
 10     P=   <B10>                 <C10>                          DET(P)
 11          <B11>                 <C11>                          (B10*C11)
                                                                  -(C10*B11)
 12
 13     P'=  +C11/E11              -C10/E11                       DOT COL
 14          -B11/E11              +B10/E11                       (B10*C10)
                                                                  +(B11*C11)
 15
 16     P'A= (B13*B3)+(C13*B4)     (B13*C3)+(C13*C4)
 17          (B14*B3)+(C14*B4)     (B14*C3)+(C14*C4)
 18
 19    P'AP= (B16*B10)+(C16*B11)   (B16*C10)+(C16*C11)
 20          (B17*B10)+(C17*B11)   (B17*C10)+(C17*C11)

  B6:  ((B3+C4)+@SQRT((B3-C4)*(B3-C4)+(4*C3*B4)))/2
  C6:  ((B3+C4)-@SQRT((B3-C4)*(B3-C4)+(4*C3*B4)))/2
  C8:  @MAX(@ABS(C3),@ABS(B4))

  B10: @IF(C8=0,1,@IF(C3=0,C4-B6,C3))
  B11: @IF(C8=0,0,@IF(C3=0,-B4,B6-B3))
  C10: @IF(C8=0,0,@IF(B6=C6,@NA,@IF(C3=0,C4-C6,C3)))
  C11: @IF(C8=0,1,@IF(B6=C6,@NA,@IF(C3=0,-B4,C6-B3)))
```

Figure 15-1   Eigenvalues and diagonalization.

For an eigenvalue λ, both $[b \quad \lambda - a]^T$ and $[d - \lambda \quad -c]^T$ are (possibly zero) eigenvectors. If λ_1 and λ_2 are eigenvalues with corresponding eigenvectors $[m_1 \quad n_1]^T$ and $[m_2 \quad n_2]^T$ which are linearly independent, set

$$P = \begin{bmatrix} m_1 & m_2 \\ n_1 & n_2 \end{bmatrix}$$

Then

$$P^{-1}AP = \begin{bmatrix} \lambda_1 & 0 \\ 1 & \lambda_2 \end{bmatrix}$$

and P diagonalizes A. The spreadsheet (Figure 15-1) determines the matrix P, if it exists, and the product $P^{-1}AP$. The columns of P are found as follows:

1. If $(a - d)^2 + 4bc < 0$, then A has no real eigenvalues and P does not exist.
2. If A is diagonal, set $P = I$ (the identity matrix).
3. If A is nondiagonal with real eigenvalues λ_1 and λ_2, A can be diagonalized if and only if $\lambda_1 \neq \lambda_2$. If $\lambda_1 \neq \lambda_2$, choose

$$\begin{bmatrix} m_i \\ n_i \end{bmatrix} = \begin{cases} \begin{bmatrix} d - \lambda_i \\ -c \end{bmatrix} & \text{if } b = 0 \\ \begin{bmatrix} b \\ \lambda_i - a \end{bmatrix} & \text{if } b \neq 0 \end{cases} \quad \text{for } i = 1, 2$$

If $\lambda_1 = \lambda_2$, choose $[m_1 \quad n_1]^T$ as above and set

$$\begin{bmatrix} m_2 \\ n_2 \end{bmatrix} = \begin{bmatrix} \text{NA} \\ \text{NA} \end{bmatrix}$$

where NA stands for not available.

If A is a symmetric matrix, that is, $b = c$, the columns of P found by this routine are orthogonal; i.e., their dot product is zero. The spreadsheet also calculates this dot product (see Exercise 15-2).

SPREADSHEET CONSTRUCTION

1. Enter the matrix A into cells $\|$B3 to C4$\|$.
2. Enter the indicated formulas for the eigenvalues into cells B6 and C6. ERROR will be shown if A has no real eigenvalues.

3. Cause 0 to appear in cell C8 if the matrix A is diagonal. Enter

$$@MAX(@ABS(C3),@ABS(B4))$$

4. Calculate P in cells $\|B10$ to $C11\|$. Compare the given formulas with cases 1 to 3 above. Note that A is a diagonal matrix if the value of cell C8 is 0. If a nondiagonal matrix A has a repeated eigenvalue, an eigenvector appears in the first column of P and NA in the second. If A has no real eigenvalues, ERROR appears throughout P.

5. Calculate the determinant of P in cell E11 and P^{-1} in cells $\|B13$ to $C14\|$;

$$P^{-1} = \frac{1}{\det P}\begin{bmatrix} n_2 & -m_2 \\ -n_1 & m_1 \end{bmatrix}$$

6. Compute the matrix products $P^{-1}A$ in $\|B16$ to $C17\|$ and $P^{-1}AP$ in $\|B19$ to $C20\|$ (see Demonstration 12).

7. Compute the dot product of the columns of P in E14. If this value is 0, then the columns are orthogonal, P is called an orthogonal matrix, and A is said to be orthogonally diagonalizable.

USER INTERACTION

Vary the matrix A in $\|B3$ to $C4\|$.

Exercises and Modifications

15-1. Use the spreadsheet to investigate the eigenvalues and eigenvectors of the following matrices and diagonalize them if possible:

a. $\begin{bmatrix} 5 & 7 \\ 7 & 0 \end{bmatrix}$ b. $\begin{bmatrix} -2 & 5 \\ 6 & 4 \end{bmatrix}$ c. $\begin{bmatrix} 0 & -1 \\ 1 & 0 \end{bmatrix}$ d. $\begin{bmatrix} 0 & 1 \\ 1 & 0 \end{bmatrix}$

15-2. If

$$\mathbf{u} = [u_1 \quad u_2 \quad \ldots \quad u_n] \quad \text{and} \quad \mathbf{v} = [v_1 \quad v_2 \quad \ldots \quad v_n]$$

then the dot product of $\mathbf{u}$ and $\mathbf{v}$ is defined by

$$\mathbf{u} \cdot \mathbf{v} = u_1v_1 + u_2v_2 + \cdots + u_nv_n$$

Create a spreadsheet to compute the dot product of vectors $\mathbf{u}$ and $\mathbf{v}$, the projection of $\mathbf{u}$ onto $\mathbf{v}$, that is, $[(\mathbf{u} \cdot \mathbf{v})/(\mathbf{v} \cdot \mathbf{v})]\mathbf{v}$, and the angle between **u** and **v**,

$$\arccos \left[\frac{\mathbf{u} \cdot \mathbf{v}}{(\mathbf{u} \cdot \mathbf{u})(\mathbf{v} \cdot \mathbf{v})} \right]$$

[53, pp. 105–107, and 55, pp. 670–671].

15-3. Use eigenvalues and eigenvectors to write the quadratic form $f(x, y) = 4x^2 + 3xy - 8y^2$ in the form $a(x')^2 + b(y')^2$ [1, pp. 281–289].

REFERENCES

Eigenvalues and eigenvectors: references 1, 24, 36, 53, and 64.

Diagonalization: references 1, 36, 46, 53, and 64.

Systems of differential equations: references 1, 11, 36, 53, 64, and 65.

Geometry applications and quadratic forms: references 1, 36, 53, and 64.

Projections: references 1, 2, 43, 53, 55, and 64.

Continued Fractions

A (simple) continued fraction is an expression of the form

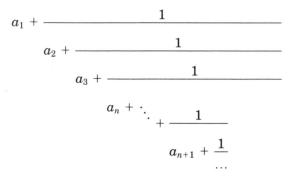

where the a_i are positive integers. This continued fraction will be denoted $[a_1; a_2; \ldots; a_n; \ldots]$. A continued fraction with repeated terms will be written

$$[3; 1; 2; 1; 2; 1; 2; 1; 2; \ldots] = [3; \overline{1; 2}]$$

Continued fractions which have finite expansions are easily evaluated; for example,

$$[1; 3; 5; 2] = 1 + \cfrac{1}{3 + 1/(5 + \frac{1}{2})}$$

$$= 1 + \cfrac{1}{3 + 2/11}$$

$$= 1 + 11/35 = 46/35$$

Infinite (or finite) continued fractions can be evaluated iteratively by defining convergents c_i

$$c_1 = a_1 \qquad c_2 = a_1 + \frac{1}{a_2} \qquad c_3 = a_1 + \frac{1}{a_2 + 1/a_3}$$

and so on. It can be shown [44, p. 21] that $c_i = p_i/q_i$, where

$$\begin{array}{lll} p_1 = a_1 & p_2 = a_1a_2 + 1 & \text{and} \\ q_1 = 1 & q_2 = a_2 & \text{and} \end{array} \qquad \begin{array}{l} p_i = a_ip_{i-1} + p_{i-2} \\ q_i = a_iq_{i-1} + q_{i-2} \end{array} \quad (16\text{-}1)$$

for $i > 2$. For a finite continued fraction

$$[a_1; \, a_2; \, \ldots \, ; \, a_n] = \frac{p_n}{q_n}$$

while the value of an infinite continued fraction is $\lim\limits_{i \to \infty} c_i = \lim\limits_{i \to \infty} (p_i/q_i)$.

Each finite continued fraction can be written using either an even or an odd number of terms, since

$$[a_1; \, a_2; \, \ldots \, ; \, a_n] = \begin{cases} [a_1; \, a_2; \, \ldots \, ; \, a_n - 1; \, 1] & \text{if } a_n > 1 \\ [a_1; \, a_2; \, \ldots \, ; \, a_{n-1} + 1] & \text{if } a_n = 1 \end{cases}$$

For example,

$$[3; \, 4; \, 5] = [3; \, 4; \, 4; \, 1] \qquad \text{and} \qquad [6; \, 1; \, 4; \, 5; \, 1] = [6; \, 1; \, 4; \, 6]$$

Finally, let $a > b$ be positive integers and $a_1, a_2, \ldots, a_n$ be the sequence of quotients which arises in Euclid's algorithm with a and b. It can be shown [44, pp. 14–16] that

$$\frac{a}{b} = [a_1; \, a_2; \, \ldots \, ; \, a_n]$$

For example,

$$\frac{512}{124} = [4; \, 7; \, 1; \, 3]$$

(see Demonstration 17).

In the spreadsheet (Figure 16-1) the convergents for a continued fraction are calculated using the recurrence relations (16-1). The value of the continued fraction is $e - 1$.

SPREADSHEET CONSTRUCTION

1. Use column A as a counter; enter $a_1, a_2, \ldots$ into column B.

2. Generate $p_1 = a_1$ in cell C5 (enter +B5), $p_2 = a_1a_2 + 1$ in cell C6 (enter +B5*B6+1), $q_1 = 1$ in cell D5 (enter 1), and $q_2 = a_2$ in cell D6 (enter +B6).

3. Use the recurrence relations (16-1) to generate p_i and q_i in columns C and D. Enter $p_3 = a_3 p_2 + p_1$ as +B7*C6+C5 into cell C7 and $q_3 = a_3 q_2 + q_1$ as +B7*D6 + D5 into cell D7. Replicate each expression (columns C and D).

4. Column E contains the convergents, $c_i = p_i/q_i$. Enter $p_1/q_1 =$ +C5/D5 into cell E5 and replicate (column E).

USER INTERACTION

Change the $[a_1; a_2; \ldots]$ in cells B5, B6, B7, ...

Exercises and Modifications

16-1. Enter $[\overline{1}] = [1; 1; 1; 1; \ldots]$ into the spreadsheet. Note that this continued fraction converges to the golden ratio and that p_i and q_i are the terms of the Fibonacci sequence (see Demonstration 1).

16-2. Observe the following using a spreadsheet:
 a. $[2; \overline{1; 1; 1; 4}] = [2; 1; 1; 1; 4; 1; 1; 1; 4; \ldots] = \sqrt{7}$
 b. $[1; \overline{2}] = [1; 2; 2; 2; 2; \ldots] = \sqrt{2}$
 c. $[1; \overline{1; 2}] = [1; 1; 2; 1; 2; 1; 2; 1; 2; \ldots] = \sqrt{3}$

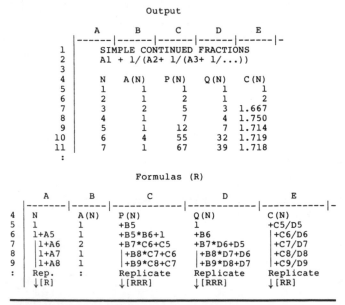

Output

	A	B	C	D	E
1		SIMPLE CONTINUED FRACTIONS			
2		A1 + 1/(A2+ 1/(A3+ 1/...))			
3					
4	N	A(N)	P(N)	Q(N)	C(N)
5	1	1	1	1	1
6	2	1	2	1	2
7	3	2	5	3	1.667
8	4	1	7	4	1.750
9	5	1	12	7	1.714
10	6	4	55	32	1.719
11	7	1	67	39	1.718
:					

Formulas (R)

	A	B	C	D	E
4	N	A(N)	P(N)	Q(N)	C(N)
5	1	1	+B5	1	+C5/D5
6	1+A5	1	+B5*B6+1	+B6	+C6/D6
7	1+A6	2	+B7*C6+C5	+B7*D6+D5	+C7/D7
8	1+A7	1	+B8*C7+C6	+B8*D7+D6	+C8/D8
9	1+A8	1	+B9*C8+C7	+B9*D8+D7	+C9/D9
:	Rep.	:	Replicate	Replicate	Replicate
	↓[R]		↓[RRR]	↓[RRR]	↓[RR]

Figure 16-1   Continued fractions for $[1; 1; 2; 1; 1; 4\ 1; 1; 6; 1; 1; 8; \ldots]$.

16-3. Modify the continued-fraction spreadsheet to calculate the values $p_k q_{k-1} - q_k p_{k-1}$. Observe that the values are $(-1)^k$ for $k = 2, 3, \ldots$

16-4. Solve the diophantine equation $167x - 74y = 1$ (x and y must be integers). *Hint:* Using Euclid's algorithm, discussed in the second paragraph following relation (16-1), above, the continued fraction for $167/74$ is

$$[2; 3; 1; 8; 2] = [2; 3; 1; 8; 1; 1]$$

Enter the expression with an even number of terms into the spreadsheet, obtaining

a_i	2	3	1	8	1	1
p_i	2	7	9	79	88	167
q_i	1	3	4	35	39	74

It can be shown that the solution of the equation is given by

$$x = 39 + 74t \qquad y = 88 + 167t \qquad t \text{ an integer}$$

In general, if $[a_1; a_2; \ldots; a_n]$, n even, is the continued fraction for a/b, $a > b$, and the greatest common divisor of a and b is 1, the general solution of $ax - by = 1$ (x and y integers) is

$$x = q_{n-1} + q_n t \qquad y = p_{n-1} + p_n t$$

Use this observation to solve the following equations in which x and y are integers:

a. $540x - 37y = 1$ b. $444x - 55y = 1$ c. $128x - 21y = 1$

For a discussion of the use of continued fractions to solve these and other diophantine equations, see Ref. 44.

REFERENCES

Continued fractions: references 7, 12, 39, 44, and 51.

Diophantine equations: references 12 and 44.

Euclid's
GCD Algorithm

The greatest common divisor (GCD) of two positive integers a and b is the largest positive integer that is a divisor, or factor, of both a and b. For example, the GCD of 12 and 15 is 3, the GCD of 20 and 70 is 10, and the GCD of 8 and 15 is 1. Euclid's algorithm, described below, is one method for finding the GCD of two integers.

Let a and b be positive integers with $a > b$. Divide a by b, obtaining a nonnegative integer quotient q_1 and an integer remainder r_1 satisfying $0 \leq r_1 < b$; that is,

$$a = q_1 b + r_1 \qquad 0 \leq r_1 < b$$

Next, if $r_1 \neq 0$, divide b by r_1 and obtain

$$b = q_2 r_1 + r_2 \qquad 0 \leq r_2 < r_1$$

Then, if $r_2 \neq 0$, divide r_1 by r_2 and obtain

$$r_1 = q_3 r_2 + r_3 \qquad 0 \leq r_3 < r_2$$

Repeat the process by dividing the previous remainder by the new remainder to find pairs of nonnegative integers q_n and r_n (quotients and remainders) satisfying

$$
\begin{aligned}
a &= q_1 b + r_1 & 0 < r_1 < b \\
b &= q_2 r_1 + r_2 & 0 < r_2 < r_1 \\
r_1 &= q_3 r_2 + r_3 & 0 < r_3 < r_2 \\
r_2 &= q_4 r_3 + r_4 & 0 < r_4 < r_3
\end{aligned}
$$

. . . .

$$r_{n-2} = q_n r_{n-1} + r_n \qquad 0 < r_n < r_{n-1}$$
$$r_{n-1} = q_{n+1} r_n + 0$$

until a zero remainder is obtained. The last nonzero remainder, r_n, is the GCD.

Example: Find the GCD of 512 and 124:

$$
\begin{array}{cccc}
4 & 7 & 1 & 3 \\
124\overline{)512} & 16\overline{)124} & 12\overline{)16} & 4\overline{)12} \\
\underline{496} & \underline{112} & \underline{12} & \underline{12} \\
16 & 12 & 4 & 0
\end{array}
$$

$$512 = 4(124) + 16$$
$$124 = 7(16) + 12$$
$$16 = 1(12) + \ \ 4$$
$$12 = 3(4) + \ \ 0$$
$$GCD = 4$$

This algorithm is implemented in the spreadsheet in Figure 17-1 using the example above. The GCD is the last nonzero number in column D.

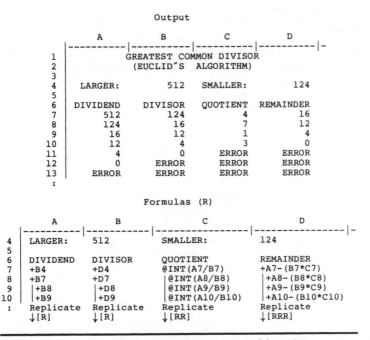

Figure 17-1 Euclid's GCD algorithm for $a = 512$ and $b = 124$.

SPREADSHEET CONSTRUCTION

1. Enter a and b into cells B4 and D4 and copy them into cells A7 and B7 as the initial dividend and divisor, respectively.

2. The dividends, divisors, quotients, and remainders are calculated at each step in columns A, B, C, and D, respectively.

   a. The quotient when a is divided by b is the greatest integer in a/b. Enter @INT(A7/B7) into cell C7.

   b. The remainder when a is divided by b is $a - b$ times the quotient. Enter +A7−(B7*C7) into cell D7.

   c. Each dividend is the previous divisor. Enter +B7 into cell A8.

   d. Each divisor is the previous remainder. Enter +D7 into cell B8.

3. For subsequent iterations, replicate the expressions in A8, B8, C7, and D7 (columns A to D).

USER INTERACTION

Change the integers a and b (cells B4 and D4).

Exercises and Modifications

17-1. Find the GCD of 1215 and 6660; then use the quotients of the spreadsheet output to find a continued fraction for 6660/1215 (see Demonstration 16).

17-2. Modify the spreadsheet to include a calculation of the least common multiple (LCM) of two integers

$$LCM(a, \ b) = \frac{ab}{GCD(a, \ b)}$$

17-3. Design a spreadsheet to determine the digits that appear in the decimal expansion of a/b, for example,

$$\frac{4}{7} : 5 \ \ 7 \ \ 1 \ \ 4 \ \ 2 \ \ 8 \ \ 5 \ \ 7 \ \ 1 \ \ 4 \ \ 2 \ \ 8 \ \ \cdots$$

* 17-4. The GCD of 187 and 221 is 17. Note that this GCD can be written as a sum of multiples of 187 and 221

$$17 = 6(187) + (-5)(221)$$

Using the fact that $r_i = r_{i-2} - q_i r_{i-1}$, create a spreadsheet which generates integers s and t so that

$$GCD(a, b) = sa + tb$$

[12, pp. 31–34].

REFERENCES

Euclid's algorithm: references 6, 12, 44, 45, and 51.

Continued fractions: references 12, 39, and 44.

18

Binomial Theorem

The binomial expansion of $(a + b)^n$ is given by

$$(a + b)^n = a^n + C_{n,1}a^{n-1}b + C_{n,2}a^{n-2}b^2 + \cdots + C_{n,i}a^{n-i}b^i + \cdots + b^n$$

where

$$C_{n,i} = \frac{n!}{i!(n-i)!} \quad n \geq i$$

It is easy to show that

$$C_{0,0}a^0b^0 = 1 \qquad C_{1,0}a^1b^0 = a \qquad C_{1,1}a^0b^1 = b$$

and that

$$C_{n,i}a^{n-i}b^i = a(C_{n-1,i}a^{n-i-1}b^i) + b(C_{n-1,i-1}a^{n-i}b^{i-1}) \qquad \text{for } n > 1$$

This recurrence relation is used in the spreadsheet (Figure 18-1) to generate the terms $C_{n,i}a^{n-i}b^i$ of the expansion of $(a + b)^n$ using $a = 2$, $b = 1$. The value of $(a + b)^n$ is found in column M as the sum of the individual terms. In the output, i denotes the exponent of b. Note that Pascal's triangle is produced when $a = b = 1$.

This spreadsheet can also be used in the study of binomial probabilities by setting $a = P(A)$ and $b = 1 - a$, where $P(A)$ is the probability of success in a single trial of a binomial experiment [32, 50]; see Exercises 18-3 to 18-5.

SPREADSHEET CONSTRUCTION

1. Enter the values of a and b into cells B3 and B4.
2. Generate a counter for n in column A beginning with 0 in cell A7

and a counter for i (the exponent of b) in row 6 beginning with 0 in cell C6.

3. Enter $C_{0,0}a^0b^0 = 1$ into cell C7; copy the value of a (+B3) into cell C8 and the value of b (+B4) into cell D8 (these give $C_{1,0}a^1b^0$ and $C_{1,1}a^0b^1$).

4. Since the (n,i)th cell generates

$$C_{n,i}a^{n-i}b^i = a(C_{n-1,i}a^{(n-1)-i}b^i) + b(C_{n-1,i-1}a^{(n-1)-(i-1)}b^{i-1})$$

enter the expression

$$(B3*\text{"cell above"})+(B4*\text{"cell above and left"})$$

into each remaining cell. Notice that since column B is left blank, this relation holds even for column C. Enter (B3*C8)+(B4*B8) into cell C9. Replicate this expression down column C; then replicate column C across rows, in each case with B3 and B4 constant and C8 and B8 relative locations.

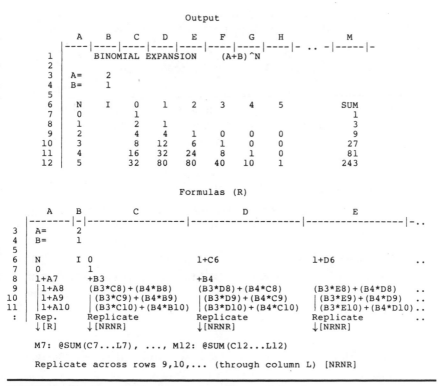

Figure 18-1 The binomial theorem for $(a + b)^n$, $a = 2$, $b = 1$.

5. To find the sum of each row, enter @SUM(C7...L7) in cell M7 and replicate (column M). Using a vertical window may enhance the display.

USER INTERACTION

1. Vary B3 and B4. Note that B3 = B4 = 1 gives Pascal's triangle.
2. Enter a number p, $0 \leqslant p \leqslant 1$, into cell B3 and change the formula in cell B4 to $1 - B3$. The resulting table produces binomial probabilities (see Exercise 18-3).

Exercises and Modifications

18-1. The numbers generated by the spreadsheet are also the coefficients of the expansion of $(ax+by)^n$. Find the expansion of $(5x-3y)^5$.

18-2. Modify the spreadsheet to find binomial expansions with $n = 6$, 7, ...

18-3. If the probability of success in one trial is p, the probability of obtaining exactly $n - i$ successes in n trials of binomial experiment is given by

$$C_{n,n-i}p^{n-i}(1 - p)^i = C_{n,i}p^{n-i}(1 - p)^i$$

Change the expression in cell B4 to $1 - B3$ and enter the value of p into cell B3. The resulting numbers in row n are thus the probabilities of obtaining exactly $n, n - 1, . . . , 2, 1, 0$ successes in n trials. Use this to solve the following problem. The probability of throwing a 2 on a die is $p = \frac{1}{6}$. Find the probability of exactly 5, 4, 3, 2, 1, 0 occurrences of a 2 in five throws of a die. (Ans: .0001, .003, .032, .161, .402, .402)

18-4. Add a row to the spreadsheet to find $P(x \geqslant n - i)$, the probability of at least $n - i$ $(n - i = 5, 4, 3, 2, 1, 0)$ successes in $n = 5$ trials of a binomial event, where x is the number of successes obtained (see Exercise 18-3).

18-5. Use the spreadsheet of Exercise 18-4 to find the expected value of x, $\mu = E(x) = \Sigma xP(x)$. Verify that $\mu = np$ [62]. Also find the variance of x

$$\sigma^2 = E[(x-\mu)^2] = \Sigma(x - \mu)^2P(x)$$

and verify that $\sigma^2 = np(1-p)$. $P(x)$ is the probability of exactly x successes.

18-6. Analyze the following problem using Exercises 18-3 to 18-5. The probability that Joe will make a free-throw shot is .8. For his next five free-throw shots find the probability of his making (a) exactly and (b) at least $n - i$ of the shots, for $n - i = 5, 4, 3, 2, 1,$ 0; (c) find the expected number of shots that will be made.

18-7. Create spreadsheets to generate Stirling numbers of the first and second kind using the relations

First: $\quad s_{0,0} = 1 \qquad s_{n,0} = s_{0,k} = 0$

$\qquad s_{n,k} = s_{n-1,k-1} + (n - 1)s_{n-1,k} \qquad$ for $n,k > 0$

Second: $\quad S_{0,0} = 1 \qquad S_{n,0} = S_{0,k} = 0$

$\qquad S_{n,k} - S_{n-1,k-1} + kS_{n-1,k} \qquad$ for $n, k > 0$

REFERENCES

Binomial coefficients: references 8, 12, 16, 19, 20, 27, 34, and 58.

Binomial probability: references 8, 10, 18, 27, 32, 40, 50, and 62.

Pascal's triangle: references 8, 12, 16, 33, and 58.

Stirling numbers: references 8, 16, and 38.

Demonstration

Synthetic Division

Synthetic division is a classical method for evaluating a polynomial

$$P(x) = p_nx^n + p_{n-1}x^{n-1} + p_{n-2}x^{n-2} + \ldots + p_1x + p_0$$

at a point $x = a$, as well as for finding the quotient $Q(x)$ and the remainder r when $P(x)$ is divided by $x - a$. The algorithm is presented using the table below.

a	p_n	p_{n-1}	p_{n-2}	$\ldots$	p_2	p_1	p_0
		c_{n-1}	c_{n-2}	$\ldots$	c_2	c_1	c_0
	q_n	q_{n-1}	q_{n-2}	$\ldots$	q_2	q_1	q_0

The sequences of q's and c's are computed as follows:

Step 1: $\quad\quad\quad\quad\quad\quad\quad\quad\quad q_n = p_n$

Step 2: $\quad\quad c_{n-1} = aq_n \quad\quad q_{n-1} = p_{n-1} + c_{n-1}$

Step 3: $\quad\quad c_{n-2} = aq_{n-1} \quad\quad q_{n-2} = p_{n-2} + c_{n-2}$

$\ldots\ldots\ldots\ldots\ldots\ldots\ldots\ldots\ldots\ldots\ldots\ldots\ldots\ldots$

Step n: $\quad\quad c_1 = aq_2 \quad\quad q_1 = p_1 + c_1$

Step $n + 1$: $\quad c_0 = aq_1 \quad\quad q_0 = p_0 + c_0$

The quotient is

$$Q(x) = q_nx^{n-1} + q_{n-1}x^{n-2} + \ldots + q_2x + q_1$$

and $P(a) = r = q_0$. If the process is repeated using $Q(x)$ in place of $P(x)$, the resulting remainder is the derivative, $P'(a)$.

The spreadsheet (Figure 19-1) shows that if $P(x) = 5x^3 + 3x^2 + 5x + 8$ is divided by $x - 2$, the resulting quotient is $Q(x) = 5x^2 + 13x + 31$, with remainder 70. In addition, $P(2) = 70$ and $P'(2) = 77$.

SPREADSHEET CONSTRUCTION

1. Enter the polynomial coefficients into cells B3 to B6 and the value of a into cell B7. Copy cell B7 into cells A9 and A15 for display. Copy the values of cells B3 to B6 into cells B9 to E9, as shown.

2. An entry in row 10 (columns C to E) is the product of a (B7) and the entry in row 12 of the previous column. Enter +B7*B12 into cell

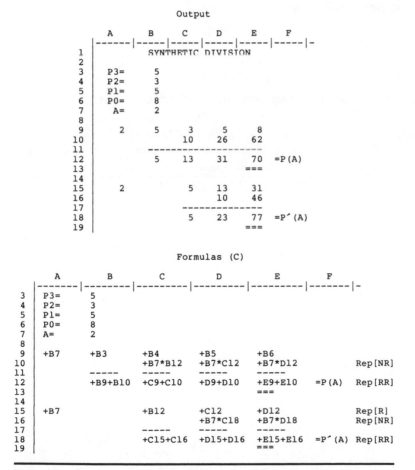

Figure 19-1 Synthetic division for $P(x) = 5x^3 + 3x^2 + 5x + 8$, $a = 2$.

C10 and replicate across row 10, with B7 a constant location and B12 relative.

3. An entry in row 12 is the sum of a given column's entries in rows 9 and 10. Enter +B9+B10 into cell B12 and replicate across row 12.

4. Copy the entries from row 12 into row 15, shifting columns by 1 to the right. Repeat steps 2 and 3 appropriately in rows 16 and 18.

USER INTERACTION

1. Change $P(x)$ by changing the coefficients in cells B3 to B6.

2. Evaluate $P(x)$ at different points $x = a$ (B7).

Exercises and Modifications

19-1. Use the synthetic-division spreadsheet to locate the roots of a polynomial by first finding an interval on which the polynomial changes signs and then continually reducing the size of that interval (see Demonstration 3). Use $P(x) = x^3 - 8x^2 + 5x + 1$.

19-2. Create a synthetic-division spreadsheet for polynomials of degree higher than 3.

* 19-3. Design a spreadsheet to carry out the long division of polynomials. You will need to modify the design of the standard long-division algorithm to take into account the order in which spreadsheet calculations are carried out.

REFERENCES

Synthetic division: references 11, 17, 19, 20, 22, 23, and 34.

Contour Graph
of $z = f(x, y)$

A *level-curve graph* of a function $z = f(x, y)$ (also called a contour graph) can readily be constructed using a spreadsheet by displaying the values of the function at points (x_i, y_j) in a rectangular grid. To accomplish this, select initial values x_0 and y_0, which establish the upper left corner of the grid, and step sizes $h > 0$, $k > 0$. Let

$$x_i = x_0 + ih \qquad y_j = y_0 + jk \qquad i, j = 1, 2, \ldots$$

and evaluate the $f(x_i, y_j)$. In the spreadsheet (Figure 20-1) values of f have been rounded to the nearest integer to improve the screen display. By changing the values x_0 and y_0 the user can observe different sections of the graph. The function used is $f(x, y) = (y - x^2)/4$.

Because the best screen output often results when columns of width 3 are used, it may be desirable to include a scaling factor, so that only single-digit integers will be generated when values for $f(x_i, y_j)$ are displayed (see Exercise 20-2).

SPREADSHEET CONSTRUCTION

1. Enter the coordinates of the upper left point of the grid (x_0, y_0) into cells B1 and B2 and x and y step sizes (h, k) into cells D1 and D2.

2. To construct the x axis, first copy x_0 (+B1) into cell C4; then compute $x_0 + h$ in cell D4 by +C4+D1. Replicate this expression into cells D4 to M4, with C4 relative and D1 constant. Construct the y axis similarly in column A.

3. Evaluate $f(x_0, y_0)$ in cell C6 using the x and y components in cells C4 and A6, rounding answer to the nearest integer: enter

$$@INT((A6-(C4*C4))/4+.5)$$

4. To evaluate f at the other points, first replicate the expression in cell C6 across row 6, with the y value (A6) constant and the x value (C4) relative. Then replicate row 6 (columns C to M) into rows 7, 8, 9, . . . with the y values relative and the x values constant.

USER INTERACTION

1. Change the initial coordinates (cells B1 and B2) to examine a different portion of the domain of the function.

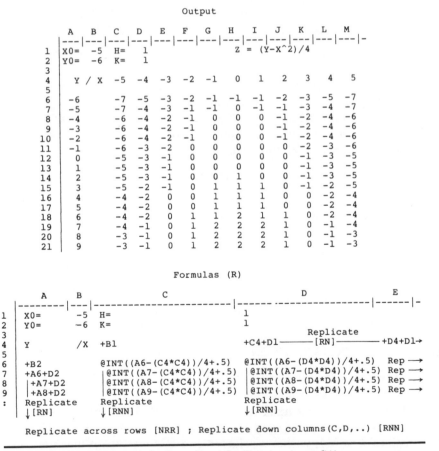

Output

	A	B	C	D	E	F	G	H	I	J	K	L	M
1	X0=	-5	H=	1				Z	=	(Y-X^2)/4			
2	Y0=	-6	K=	1									
3													
4	Y / X	-5	-4	-3	-2	-1	0	1	2	3	4	5	
5													
6	-6	-7	-5	-3	-2	-1	-1	-1	-2	-3	-5	-7	
7	-5	-7	-4	-3	-1	-1	0	-1	-1	-3	-4	-7	
8	-4	-6	-4	-2	-1	0	0	0	-1	-2	-4	-6	
9	-3	-6	-4	-2	-1	0	0	0	-1	-2	-4	-6	
10	-2	-6	-4	-2	-1	0	0	0	-1	-2	-4	-6	
11	-1	-6	-3	-2	0	0	0	0	0	-2	-3	-6	
12	0	-5	-3	-1	0	0	0	0	0	-1	-3	-5	
13	1	-5	-3	-1	0	0	0	0	0	-1	-3	-5	
14	2	-5	-3	-1	0	0	1	0	0	-1	-3	-5	
15	3	-5	-2	-1	0	1	1	1	0	-1	-2	-5	
16	4	-4	-2	0	0	1	1	1	0	0	-2	-4	
17	5	-4	-2	0	0	1	1	1	0	0	-2	-4	
18	6	-4	-2	0	1	1	2	1	1	0	-2	-4	
19	7	-4	-1	0	1	2	2	2	1	0	-1	-4	
20	8	-3	-1	0	1	2	2	2	1	0	-1	-3	
21	9	-3	-1	0	1	2	2	2	1	0	-1	-3	

Formulas (R)

	A	B	C	D	E
1	X0=	-5	H=		1	
2	Y0=	-6	K=		1	
3					Replicate	
4	Y	/X	+B1	+C4+D1————[RN]————+D4+D1→		
5						
6	+B2	@INT((A6-(C4*C4))/4+.5)	@INT((A6-(D4*D4))/4+.5)	Rep →		
7	+A6+D2	@INT((A7-(C4*C4))/4+.5)	@INT((A7-(D4*D4))/4+.5)	Rep →		
8	+A7+D2	@INT((A8-(C4*C4))/4+.5)	@INT((A8-(D4*D4))/4+.5)	Rep →		
9	+A8+D2	@INT((A9-(C4*C4))/4+.5)	@INT((A9-(D4*D4))/4+.5)	Rep →		
:	Replicate	Replicate	Replicate			
	↓[RN]	↓[RNN]	↓[RNN]			

Replicate across rows [NRR] ; Replicate down columns (C,D,..) [RNN]

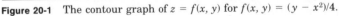

Figure 20-1 The contour graph of $z = f(x, y)$ for $f(x, y) = (y - x^2)/4$.

2. Decrease h and k (cells D1 and D2) to enlarge a portion of the graph.

Exercises and Modifications

20-1. Modify the spreadsheet to produce graphs of the following functions:

   a. $f(x, y) = \dfrac{0.5x^2 + 2y^2}{12}$ b. $f(x, y) = \dfrac{x^2 - y^2}{3}$

20-2. We must be able to examine graphs of functions for which values of $f(x, y)$ are too large to display on the screen (resulting in a display of >>>). To overcome this difficulty, include a scaling factor in the spreadsheet. For example, enter a positive number, say .5, into cell F1. Replace the expression for the function in cell C7 by

$$@INT(F1*((A6-(C4*C4))/4)+.5)$$

and replicate this in the same manner as in the original construction. The values shown will be values of $f(x, y)$ scaled by a factor of 0.5.

20-3. Use the ideas of this section to construct a similar "graph" consisting of a single row for a function of one variable, for example, $f(x) = x^2$, $-4 \leqslant x \leqslant 4$.

REFERENCES

Contour (level-curve) graphs: references 2 and 43.

Demonstration

Modular Arithmetic

Let n be a positive integer. The sum modulo n of two integers a and b is the nonnegative remainder $(0, 1, 2, . . ., n - 1)$ that results when $a + b$ is divided by n. For example, $5 + 6 = 4$ modulo 7, since when 11 is divided by 7 the remainder is 4. Multiplication modulo n is defined similarly, and $5(6) = 2$ modulo 7 [42]. The set of integers modulo n is the set $\{0, 1, 2, . . ., n - 2, n - 1\}$ together with the above operations. This demonstration shows how a spreadsheet can be used to generate addition and multiplication tables for the integers modulo n, where the user enters a value for n, $n \leq 7$. The result for $n = 5$ is shown in Figure 21-1. This implementation assumes the use of a spreadsheet column width of 3 (see Exercise 21-1 for a different approach).

SPREADSHEET CONSTRUCTION

1. Set the column width to 3, so that when the value of a cell is 9999, the symbol $>>>$ will be displayed.
2. Enter a value for n (1, 2, . . . , 7) into cell B1.
3. Generate integers 0, 1, 2, . . . , 6 (but none exceeding $n - 1$) across row 2. Enter 0 into cell C2 and @IF(C2+1<B1,C2+1,9999) into cell D2. If C2+1 is as large as n, then $>>>$ will be displayed. Replicate the expression in cell D2 into cells E2 to I2 with C2 relative and B1 constant.
4. Repeat the process of step 3 in column A, from A4 to A10. Then copy row 2 into row 12 and cells A4 to A10 into cells A14 to A20.

Output

	A	B	C	D	E	F	G	H	I
1	N=	5							
2	+		0	1	2	3	4	>>>	>>>
3			....						
4	0	.	0	1	2	3	4	>>>	>>>
5	1	.	1	2	3	4	0	>>>	>>>
6	2	.	2	3	4	0	1	>>>	>>>
7	3	.	3	4	0	1	2	>>>	>>>
8	4	.	4	0	1	2	3	>>>	>>>
9	>>>	.	>>>	>>>	>>>	>>>	>>>	>>>	>>>
10	>>>	.	>>>	>>>	>>>	>>>	>>>	>>>	>>>
11									
12	*		0	1	2	3	4	>>>	>>>
13			....						
14	0	.	0	0	0	0	0	>>>	>>>
15	1	.	0	1	2	3	4	>>>	>>>
16	2	.	0	2	4	1	3	>>>	>>>
17	3	.	0	3	1	4	2	>>>	>>>
18	4	.	0	4	3	2	1	>>>	>>>
19	>>>	.	>>>	>>>	>>>	>>>	>>>	>>>	>>>
20	>>>	.	>>>	>>>	>>>	>>>	>>>	>>>	>>>

Formulas (R)

	A	B	C	D	E	I
1	N=	5				
2	+		0	@IF(C2+1<B1, C2+1,9999)	@IF(D2+1<B1, D2+1,9999)	... @IF(H2+1<B1, H2+1,9999)
3		.	....	....		
4	0	.	<C4>	<D4>	< >	<I4>
5	<A5>	.	|<C5>	|<D5>	|< >	|< >
6	|<A6>	.	|<C6>	|<D6>	|< >	|< >
:	Rep.	.	Rep.	Rep.	Rep.	Rep.
:	|[RNR]	.	|[..]	|[..]	|[..]	|[..]
10	↓<A10>	.	↓<C10>	↓<D10>	↓<E10>	↓<I10>
11						
12	*		+C2	+D2	+E2	+I2
13		.	....	....		
14	+A4	.	<C14>	<D14>	<E14>	<I14>
15	|+A5	.	|<C15>	|<D15>	|<E15>	|<I15>
:	Rep.	.	Rep.	Rep.	Rep.	Rep.
:	|[R]	.	|[..]	|[..]	|[..]	|[..]
20	↓+A10	.	↓<C20>	↓<D20>	↓<E20>	↓<I20>

```
C4:   @IF(@OR(C2>99,A4>99),9999,A4+C2-(B1*@INT((A4+C2)/B1)))
D4:   @IF(@OR(D2>99,A4>99),9999,A4+D2-(B1*@INT((A4+D2)/B1)))
  :
I4:   @IF(@OR(I2>99,A4>99),9999,A4+I2-(B1*@INT((A4+I2)/B1)))

C10:  @IF(@OR(C2>99,A10>99),9999,A10+C2-(B1*@INT((A10+C2)/B1)))
  :
I10:  @IF(@OR(I2>99,A10>99),9999,A10+I2-(B1*@INT((A10+I2)/B1)))

A5:   @IF(A4+1<B1,A4+1,9999)    ...    A10:  @IF(A9+1<B1,A9+1,9999)

C14:  @IF(@OR(C12>99,A14>99),9999,A14*C12-(B1*@INT((A14*C12)/B1)))

Replicate across row 2: [RNR]
Replication in main body of table: Across rows:   [RNNRNNRN]
                                   Down columns:  [NRRNNRNN]
```

Figure 21-1 Modular arithmetic.

5. The sum modulo n of x and y is the remainder when $x + y$ is divided by n

$$x + y - n \text{ int} \left(\frac{x + y}{n} \right)$$

where int is the greatest integer function. Enter

@IF(@OR(C2>99,A4>99),9999,A4+C2−(B1*@INT((A4+C2)/B1)))

into cell C4. If either C2 or A4 is 9999, >>> will be displayed.

6. Replicate the expression in cell C4 across row 4, with the column location (C2) relative and the row location (A4) constant. Then replicate row 4 (columns C to I) into rows 5 to 10 with the column locations constant and the row locations relative.

7. Repeat steps 3 to 5 in rows 14 to 20, using C14 as the initial cell, replacing addition (+) by multiplication (*) in each expression.

USER INTERACTION

Change n (cell B1) to 1, 2, . . . , 7 to generate new tables.

Exercises and Modifications

21-1. Create a simpler spreadsheet for the example by causing NA to appear in place of >>>. Enter @IF(C2+1<B1,C2+1,@NA) in cell D2. If similar formulas are used in rows 4 and 14 and column A, formulas such as

+A4+C2−(B1*(@INT((A4+C2)/B1)))

in cell C4 can be used in the body of the tables.

21-2. Create spreadsheets to generate modular arithmetic tables for $n > 7$.

21-3. Create a spreadsheet to find the powers of x (x^i) modulo n for $0 \leq x < n$ and $i = 1, 2, 3, . . . , n - 1$. For example, for $n = 7, x = 3$

i	1	2	3	4	5	6
x^i	3	2	6	4	5	1

21-4. Modify Exercise 3 to compute ix, the multiples of x modulo n, for $0 \leq x < n$ and $i = 0, 1, 2, . . . , n - 1$.

REFERENCES

Modular arithmetic: references 42 and 51.

Russian Peasant Multiplication

The *Russian peasant multiplication algorithm* (also called *mediation and duplication*) provides a simple means for calculating the product of two numbers. Despite its name, the algorithm has been used by different peoples throughout history. To follow the algorithm, examine the computation of 109(234) described below and illustrated in the spreadsheet (Figure 22-1).

Create two columns; column A is headed by the smaller number (109) and column B by the larger number (234). Begin by dividing 109 by 2 (dropping the remainder) to obtain 54, and doubling 234 to obtain 468. Next divide 54 by 2 to obtain 27, and double 468 to obtain 936. Continue in this manner, dividing entries in column A by 2 (dropping any remainder) and doubling entries in column B, until 1 is reached in column A. Finally, add all the numbers in column B that occur next to *odd* entries (109, 27, 13, 3, 1) in column A. The sum obtained is the desired product.

SPREADSHEET CONSTRUCTION

1. Enter the smaller number into cell A4 and the larger into cell B4 and copy them into cells A6 and B6.
2. Each entry in column A is half the entry in the cell above it, with any remainder dropped. Enter @INT(A6/2) into cell A7 and replicate (column A).
3. Each entry in column B is twice the entry in the cell above it. Enter 2*B6 into cell B7 and replicate (column B).

4. To determine whether an entry in column A is odd or even, divide it by 2 and obtain a remainder of 1 (odd) or 0 (even). Enter +A6−(2*@INT(A6/2)) into cell C6 and replicate (column C).

5. By multiplying a number in column B by the corresponding entry in column C (either 1 or 0) one obtains either the number or 0. Enter +B6*C6 into cell D6 and replicate (column D).

6. The product is the sum of all entries in column D. Enter @SUM(D6...D13) into cell D15.

USER INTERACTION

Change the numbers to be multiplied (cells A4 and B4).

Exercises and Modifications

22-1. Carry out the following multiplications using the Russian peasant algorithm:

  a. 97(421)   b. 13(67)   c. 16(51)
  d. 32(51)   e. 64(51)

```
                        Output

                 A         B         C         D
        |---------|---------|---------|---------|-
     1  |     RUSSIAN PEASANT MULTIPLICATION
     2  |
     3  | SMALLER    LARGER
     4  |    109       234   <--ENTER
     5  |
     6  |    109       234        1        234
     7  |     54       468        0          0
     8  |     27       936        1        936
     9  |     13      1872        1       1872
    10  |      6      3744        0          0
    11  |      3      7488        1       7488
    12  |      1     14976        1      14976
    13  |      0     29952        0          0
    14  |
    15  |                    PRODUCT=      25506
```

```
                     Formulas (R)

             A            B              C                    D
        |--------------|-------|-----------------------|----------------|-
     4  | 109            234
     5  |
     6  | +A4            +B4     +A6-(2*@INT(A6/2))       +B6*C6
     7  | @INT(A6/2)     2*B6    |+A7-(2*@INT(A7/2))      |+B7*C7
     8  | |@INT(A7/2)    |2*B7   |+A8-(2*@INT(A8/2))      |+B8*C8
     :  | Replicate      Rep.    Replicate                Rep.
     :  | |[R]           |[R]    |[RR]                     |[RR]
    13  | ↓@INT(A12/2)   ↓2*B12  ↓+A13-(2*@INT(A13/2))    ↓+B13*C13
    14  |
    15  |                        PRODUCT=                 @SUM(D6...D13)
```

Figure 22-1 Russian peasant multiplication.

22-2. Notice that the integers in column C correspond to the binary (base 2) representation of the integer in cell A4. Thus, columns A and C generate the binary expansion of an integer. Design a spreadsheet in a similar fashion to find the base 3, base 4, . . . , expansions of an integer (each digit appears in a separate cell).

22-3. Create a spreadsheet to convert a decimal (base 10) integer n to a form that "looks like" the binary (base 2) and octal (base 8) expansions of n (for n not too large). For example, for the integer 5, cause the integer 101 (which looks like the binary expansion of 5) to be printed in a cell.

22-4. Egyptian fractions. The ancient Egyptians employed only fractions with numerators of 1; for example, $1/6$, $1/13$, ... Any fraction not of the form $1/n$ was written as a sum of the form

$$\frac{1}{r_1} + \frac{1}{r_2} + \cdots + \frac{1}{r_n}$$

where no term is repeated. Thus, $2/3 = 1/2 + 1/6$ (not $1/3 + 1/3$). The following algorithm will convert a fraction of the form p/q, with $p < q$, into an Egyptian fraction $1/r_1 + 1/r_2 + 1/r_3 + \cdots + 1/r_n$, where the r_i are distinct positive integers.

Let $p_1 = p$ and $q_1 = q$.

For $i \geq 1$ if $\dfrac{q_i}{p_i}$ is an integer

then $r_i = \dfrac{q_i}{p_i}$ and the process ends

else $r_i = \text{int}\left(\dfrac{q_i}{p_i}\right) + 1$ $p_{i+1} = p_i r_i - q_i$

and $q_{i+1} = q_i r_i$

Create a spreadsheet to find the r_i of the Egyptian fraction expansion for p/q.

22-5. Create a spreadsheet to illustrate the use of logarithms to do multiplication:

$3456 \rightarrow$	3.53857	Find log
$\times 123 \rightarrow$	$+2.08991$	Find log
	5.62848	Add logs
$425088 \leftarrow$		Find 10^x

REFERENCES

Russian Peasant multiplication: references 7, 21, 45, and 52.

Binary and base n numerals: references 6, 9, 39, and 42.

Egyptian fractions: references 6 and 22a.

Logarithms: references 19, 33, 34, and 63.

Statistics
Mean,
Correlation,
and
Regression

For a sample of n data points $x_1, x_2, \ldots, x_n$, two useful statistics are

$$\text{Mean} \quad \bar{x} = \frac{\Sigma x}{n}$$

$$\text{and Standard deviation} \quad s = \sqrt{\frac{n\Sigma x^2 - (\Sigma x)^2}{n(n-1)}}$$

In addition, for a sample of n pairs of data points, $(x_1, y_1), (x_2, y_2), \ldots, (x_n, y_n)$, the *Pearson correlation coefficient* is defined by

$$r = \frac{n\Sigma(xy) - (\Sigma x)(\Sigma y)}{n(n-1)s_x s_y}$$

where s_x and s_y are the standard deviations of the x and y components, respectively. The equation of the least-squares regression line, $Y = mx + b$, is obtained from

$$m = \frac{n(\Sigma xy) - (\Sigma x)(\Sigma y)}{n(\Sigma x^2) - (\Sigma x)^2} \qquad b = \bar{y} - m\bar{x}$$

where $\bar{x}$ and $\bar{y}$ are the means of the x and y components. Note that a capital Y is used to represent the line of least-squares regression and that Y_i are values on that line corresponding to the data values x_i.

The spreadsheet (Figure 23-1) is designed to accept the data, compute the values of the statistics, and display the results so that the effects of modifying the data can readily be observed. For a discussion of the concepts and their applications, see Refs. 41 and 62.

For a set of data points $\{(x_i, y_i)\}$, the least-squares regression line is the line $Y = mx + b$ which best fits the data, in the sense that

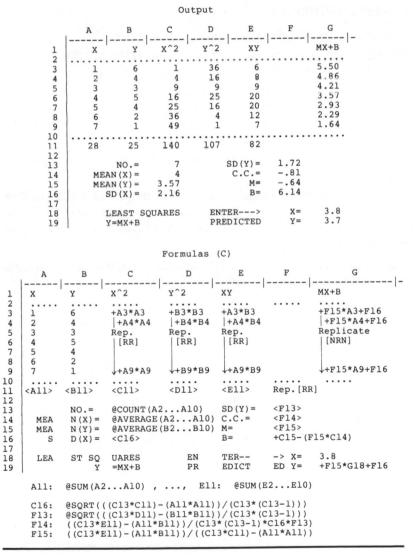

Figure 23-1 Mean, correlation, and regression.

$\Sigma(y_i - Y_i)^2$, the sum of the squares of the differences between the observed values y_i and the corresponding values $Y_i = mx_i + b$ on the line, is a minimum (see Figure 23-2). In the spreadsheet column G displays the Y_i. The least-squares line can be used to predict a value of y corresponding to other values of x as well. This is carried out in cells G18 and G19.

SPREADSHEET CONSTRUCTION

1. Enter the x, y data points into cells ‖A3 to B9‖.

2. Compute x_1^2 in cell C3 ($+$A3*A3), y_1^2 in cell D3 ($+$B3*B3), and x_1y_1 in cell E3 ($+$A3*B3). Replicate these expressions into cells ‖C4 to E9‖.

3. Find the sums of columns A to E in row 11. Enter @SUM(A2...A10) into cell A11; then replicate the expression into cells B11 to E11 (including A2 and A10 makes it easier to insert additional data).

4. Enter the expressions to compute the indicated statistics into cells ‖C13 to F16‖.

5. Using the coefficients m and b calculated in F15 and F16, find in column G the least-squares Y_i for each x_i listed in the data. Since $Y_i = mx_i + b$, enter $+$F15*A3$+$F16 into cell G3 and replicate (column G).

6. Enter a value for x into cell G18 and compute the corresponding least-squares Y in cell G19 using $+$F15*G18$+$F16.

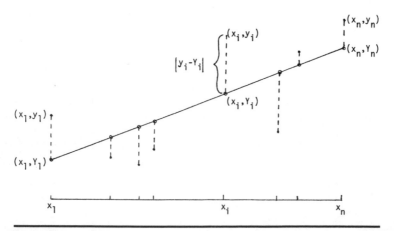

Figure 23-2   Least-squares line.

USER INTERACTION

1. Change data points ‖A3 to B9‖. Observe the effects on the computed statistics.

2. Insert additional data between rows 2 and 10. Note that this requires modification of columns C, D, E, and G, which can be done by replicating the formulas of an existing row.

3. Vary x (G18) and obtain the least-squares approximation for the predicted corresponding values of y.

Exercises and Modifications

23-1. On graph paper plot the data points ‖A3 to B9‖ together with the least-squares line obtained by using the Y_i values (cells G3 to G9).

23-2. Change the entry in cells B3 to B9 and observe the change in the mean, the correlation coefficient, the least-squares equation, etc.

23-3. Consult statistics books for similar problems. Here is an example. A survey of 10 western towns showed the following data concerning the number of taverns and churches in the towns:

Churches	3	5	6	6	7	9	10	10	11	14
Taverns	4	8	5	9	9	12	11	13	15	16

Find the means, standard deviations, least-squares line, and coefficient of correlation between the number of churches and the number of taverns. If a certain western town has eight churches, predict the number of taverns it will have.

23-4. Examine statistics texts for definitions of other correlation coefficients, e.g. Spearman's rank correlation coefficient [41, p. 507], and create spreadsheets to compute them.

23-5. Modify your spreadsheet so that each x value of the data can be multiplied by a constant. Observe the effect this coding has upon the computed values.

REFERENCES

Statistics: references 32, 41, 50, and 62.

Least-squares line: references 23, 30, 32, 41, 59, and 62.

Statistics
Confidence
Intervals

A major objective of inferential statistics is to construct confidence intervals for population parameters based on sample statistics. A typical example is the construction of a confidence interval for the mean of a normal population based on a small sample $\{x_1, x_2, \ldots, x_n\}$ of size $n < 30$. The spreadsheet in this example produces such an interval from samples of size $n \leqslant 11$ using Student's t distribution. For a discussion of the theory, see Refs. 41 and 62.

This demonstration also illustrates the use of the @LOOKUP function to read values from a table embedded in a spreadsheet.

The $c \cdot 100\%$ confidence interval for the population mean μ from a sample of $n < 30$ points is given by (for $0 < C < 1$)

$$\bar{x} - \frac{t_{\alpha/2}s}{\sqrt{n}} < \mu < \bar{x} + \frac{t_{\alpha/2}s}{\sqrt{n}}$$

where $\bar{x}$ and s are the sample mean and standard deviation, respectively, $\alpha = 1 - c$, and $t_{\alpha/2}$ comes from the t distribution with $n - 1$ degrees of freedom (Figure 24-1). For example, for a sample of size $n = 9$ with mean 20 and standard deviation 4, a 95% confidence interval ($c = 0.95$) is given by

$$20 - \frac{2.306 \, (4)}{3} < \mu < 20 + \frac{2.306 \, (4)}{3} \quad \text{or} \quad 16.93 < \mu < 23.07$$

since the value for $t_{0.025}$ with 8 degrees of freedom is 2.306. The spreadsheet (Figure 24-2) allows a user to enter sample values of x and a level of confidence ($c = 0.9, 0.95, 0.99$ only). The spreadsheet finds the sample mean and standard deviation, and a $c \cdot 100\%$ confidence interval for the population mean. The sample used is {5, 3, 8, 5, 7, 2, 7, 10}.

SPREADSHEET CONSTRUCTION

1. Enter the data points x_i into cells A5 to A12, compute x_i^2 in cells B5 to B12, calculate the values of the various statistics in cells B14 to B18 using the formulas from Demonstration 23, and enter a confidence level (0.9, 0.95, or 0.99) into cell B2.

2. The number of degrees of freedom is $n - 1$; enter $+$B16$-$1 into cell B19.

3. Enter a portion of the table of the t distribution into ∥D16 to N18∥ as indicated (consult a statistics text for a table); use row 14 for the number of degrees of freedom.

4. Copy the confidence level ($+$B2) into cell D15. If the entry in D15 matches the entry in D16, D17, or D18, the corresponding row will be copied into row 15 (see formulas).

5. Use the @LOOKUP function to match the number of degrees of freedom (B19) with an entry in row 14 and read the corresponding $t_{\alpha/2}$ value in row 15. Multiply this by $\dfrac{s}{\sqrt{n}}$, where s is the standard deviation and n the sample size, to obtain the width of the confidence interval. Enter

$$+B18*@LOOKUP(B19,E14...N14)/@SQRT(B16)$$

into cell B20.

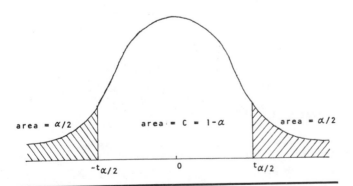

Figure 24-1 The t probability distribution.

6. Convert B2 into a percent; enter 100*B2 into cell A22. Copy the degrees of freedom (+B19) into cell B24. Compute the left (+B17−B20) and right (+B17+B20) endpoints of the confidence interval in cells A26 and C26.

```
        Output (columns A-C)              Formulas (columns A-C) (R)

         A         B        C                A          B          C
    |---------|---------|---------|-      |----------|----------|---------|-
 1  | CONFIDENCE INTERVAL                1 | CONFIDENCE INTERVAL
 2  | LEVEL        .95                   2 | LEVEL=      .95
 3  |    X        X^2                    3 | X           X^2
 4  |...............                     4 | ......      ......
 5  |    5         25                    5 | 5           +A5*A5
 6  |    3         36                    6 | 3           |+A6*A6
 7  |    8         64                    7 | 8           Replicate
 :  |    :         :                     : | :           |[RR]
12  |   10        100                   12 | 10          ↓+A12*A12
13  |...............                    13 | ......      ......
    ////////////////////////////////
14  | SUM-X       47                    14 | SUM-X       @SUM(A4...A13)   ..
15  | SUM-X^2    325                    15 | SUM-X^2     @SUM(B4...B13)   ..
16  | COUNT        8                    16 | COUNT       @COUNT(A4...A13) ..
17  | MEAN      5.875                   17 | MEAN        +B14/B16         ..
18  | SD        2.642                   18 | SD          <B18>
19  | DF           7                    19 | DF          +B16-1           ..
20  | INTV.     2.209                   20 | INTV.       <B20>            ..
21  |                                   21 |
    ////////////////////////////////
22  |      95 % CONFIDENCE INTV.        22 | 100*B2      % CONFIDENCE INT.
23  |                                   23 |
24  | T DIST           7   D.F.         24 | T DIST.     +B19        D.F.
25  |                                   25 |
26  | 3.66557  < MEAN <   8.08443       26 | +B17-B20  < MEAN <    +B17+B20
```

B18: @SQRT(((B16*B15)-(B14*B14))/(B16*(B16-1)))
B20: +B18*@LOOKUP(B19,E14...N14)/@SQRT(B16)

```
                    Output (columns D-N)

          D         E         F         G    ...      N
     |--------|--------|--------|--------|- - -|--------|-
 14  |             1        2        3    ...     10
 15  |   .95    12.706    4.303    3.182  ...    2.228
 16  |   .90     6.314    2.920    2.353  ...    1.812
 17  |   .95    12.706    4.303    3.182  ...    2.228
 18  |   .99    63.657    9.925    5.841  ...    3.169
```

```
                   Formulas (columns D-N) (R)

          D         E         F         G    ...      N
     |-------|--------|--------|--------|- - -|--------|-
 14  |            1      1+E14 — 1+F14 ————— 1+M14 — Replicate→[R]
 15  |  +B2    <E15> — <F15> — <G15> ———...— <N15> — Replicate→
 16  |  .9     6.314    2.920    2.353   •...   1.812    [NNRNNRNNR]
 17  |  .95   12.706    4.303    3.182   ...    2.228
 18  |  .99   63.657    9.925    5.841   ...    3.169
```

E15: @IF(D16=D15,E16,@IF(D15=D17,E17,@IF(D15=D18,E18,@NA)))
F15: @IF(D16=D15,F16,@IF(D15=D17,F17,@IF(D15=D18,F18,@NA)))
...
N15: @IF(D16=D15,N16,@IF(D15=D17,N17,@IF(D15=D18,N18,@NA)))

Figure 24-2 Confidence intervals.

USER INTERACTION

1. Select a confidence level of 0.9, 0.95, or 0.99 (cell B2).
2. Change the data in cells A5 to A12.
3. Delete or insert values of x_i between A4 and A13. Note that the addition formulas @SUM(A4...A13) and @SUM(B4...B13) include the lines represented by the dots, so that insertions between the lines will be included in the sum. Column B must be updated for insertions.

Exercises and Modifications

24-1. Change the values of x_i (cells A5 to A12) and observe the resulting changes in the confidence interval.

24-2. Change the confidence level (B2) to 0.9 and 0.99.

24-3. The lengths of seven hotdogs selected at random from the daily output of a local meat plant were found to be 13.6, 14.1, 13.2, 13.9, 14.0, 13.7, and 13.6 centimeters. Find a 95% confidence interval for the mean length of hotdogs produced that day at the plant.

24-4. Compare the confidence intervals for the mean constructed from the following two sets of data:
a. {1, 1, 2, 2, 2}   b. {1, 1, 1, 1, 2, 2, 2, 2, 2, 2}

24-5. Enlarge the t table to include additional confidence levels or larger samples.

24-6. Create spreadsheets to generate confidence intervals for other parameters which use the t distribution, such as the difference of the means of two populations.

24-7. Embed part of a chi-squared table into a spreadsheet and generate confidence intervals for the population variance.

24-8. Embed part of the standard normal table into a spreadsheet and generate confidence intervals for the population mean when the input data consist of the sample mean, the standard deviation, and the sample size rather than the sample points themselves.

REFERENCES

Confidence intervals and distributions: references 32, 41, and 62.

Probability
Bayes'
Rule

Bayes' rule is a fundamental result in conditional probability [27, 40]. Suppose that two successive experiments, I and II, are carried out and that experiment I has three possible outcomes a_1, a_2, a_3, with probabilities $P(a_1)$, $P(a_2)$, and $P(a_3)$. Suppose further that experiment II also has three possible outcomes b_1, b_2, b_3, and that the conditional probabilities $P(b_i|a_j)$, that is, the probability of b_i given that a_j has occurred, are known. Bayes' rule gives the reverse conditional probabilities, the probabilities of a_j given that b_i has occurred:

$$P(a_j|b_i) = \frac{P(a_j)P(b_i|a_j)}{P(b_i)}$$

where

$$P(b_i) = P(a_1)P(b_i|a_1) + P(a_2)P(b_i|a_2) + P(a_3)P(b_i|a_3)$$

To examine the concepts involved, consider the following example:

> Urn 1 contains 5 red, 0 white, and 5 blue balls.
> Urn 2 contains 5 red, 2 white, and 4 blue balls.
> Urn 3 contains 5 red, 3 white, and 2 blue balls.

An urn is chosen according to the probabilities $P(1) = .5$, $P(2) = .1$, $P(3) = .4$, and a ball is selected from that urn. The probability that the ball selected will be red, for example, is found by

$$P(R) = P(1)P(R|1)+P(2)P(R|2)+P(3)P(R|3)$$
$$= .5\,(5/10)+.1\,(5/11)+.4\,(5/10)$$
$$\approx .4955$$

Bayes' rule then gives the probability that the ball came from urn 1 given that it is red:

$$P(1|R) = \frac{P(1)P(R|1)}{P(R)}$$

$$= \frac{.5\,(.5)}{.4955}$$

$$\approx .5046$$

The spreadsheet (Figure 25-1) carries out similar computations. For example, the probability $P(W\&2)$ that the ball is white and comes from urn 2 is .0182; the probability $P(W)$ of selecting a white ball is .1382; and the probability $P(2|W)$ that the ball comes from urn 2 given that it is white is .1316.

SPREADSHEET CONSTRUCTION

1. Enter probabilities $P(1)$ and $P(2)$ into cells B3 and C3 and $1-B3-C3$ into cell D3; enter the number of balls in the urns into cells ‖B6 to D8‖.
2. Find the total numbers of balls in each urn using cells B10 to D10; for example, enter @SUM(B6...B8) into cell B10.
3. Compute joint probabilities in cells ‖B13 to D15‖; for example, the probability of a ball's being red *and* from urn 1 is

$$P(R\&1) = P(1)P(R|1)$$

where $P(R|1)$ is the number of red balls in urn 1 divided by the number of balls in urn 1. Enter +B3*B6/B10 into cell B13. Fill the other cells similarly, either directly or using replication.

4. Find $P(R)$, $P(W)$, $P(B)$ by adding the rows; for example,

$$P(R) = P(R\&1) + P(R\&2) + P(R\&3)$$

Enter

@SUM(B13...D13), ..., @SUM(B15...D15)

into cells F13 to F15.

5. Use Bayes' rule to find conditional probabilities, for example,

$$P(1|R) = \frac{P(1\&R)}{P(R)}$$

Enter +B13/F13 into cell B18. Complete cells ∥B18 to D20∥ similarly.

USER INTERACTION

1. Vary the number of balls in the urns (cells ∥B6 to D8∥).

Output

	A	B	C	D	E	F
1		BAYES PROBABILITY				
2						
3	PROB->	.5	.1	.4		
4		URN 1	URN 2	URN 3		
5						
6	RED	5	5	5		
7	WHITE	0	2	3		
8	BLUE	5	4	2		
9						
10	TOTAL	10	11	10		
11						
12	JOINT:				TOTAL:	
13	RED &	.25	.0455	.2	RED	.4955
14	WHITE&	0	.0182	.12	WHITE	.1382
15	BLUE &	.25	.0364	.08	BLUE	.3664
16						
17	CONDITIONAL:					
18	/RED	.5046	.0917	.4037		
19	/WHITE	0	.1316	.8684		
20	/BLUE	.6824	.0993	.2184		

Formulas (R)

	A	B	C	D	E	F
3	PROB->	.5	.1	1-B3-C3		
4		URN 1	URN 2	URN 3		
5						
6	RED	5	5	5		
7	WHITE	0	2	3		
8	BLUE	5	4	2		
9						
10	TOTAL	@SUM(B6...B8)	@SUM(C6...C8)	@SUM(D6...D8)		
11						
12	JOINT:				TOTAL:	
13	RED &	+B3*B6/B10	+C3*C6/C10	+D3*D6/D10	RED	@SUM(B13...D13)
14	WHITE&	+B3*B7/B10	+C3*C7/C10	+D3*D7/D10	WHITE	@SUM(B14...D14)
15	BLUE &	+B3*B8/B10	+C3*C8/C10	+D3*D8/D10	BLUE	@SUM(B15...D15)
16						
17	CONDITIONAL:					
18	/RED	+B13/F13	+C13/F13	+D13/F13		
19	/WHITE	+B14/F14	+C14/F14	+D14/F14		
20	/BLUE	+B15/F15	+C15/F15	+D15/F15		

Figure 25-1 Probability: Bayes' rule.

2. Change probabilities $P(1)$ and $P(2)$ (cells B3 and C3); once these have been set, $P(3)$ is determined.

Exercises and Modifications

25-1. Committee A consists of 2 Democrats, 6 Republicans, and 1 Independent. The corresponding compositions of committees B and C are 5, 2, 4 and 1, 2, 6. A jar contains 3 balls labeled A, 5 labeled B, and 2 labeled C. A ball is selected at random from the jar, and a person is chosen at random from the committee matching the ball. Find all the joint and conditional probabilities. What is the probability that a Republican is selected? If the person selected is a Republican, what is the probability that the person is on committee A?

25-2. Create a spreadsheet to implement Bayes' rule with n, m outcomes for the experiments when $n = 2$, $m = 4$; when $n = 3$, $m = 3$; . . . .

25-3. Create a spreadsheet to implement Bayes' rule for problems having a series of three (or more) experiments.

REFERENCES

Conditional probability and Bayes' rule: references 10, 18, 27, 32, 40, 41, 50, 62, and 63.

Algebra
Word
Problems

The information given in a word problem in algebra can often be set up in the form of a table, with variables representing unknown quantities. The usual solution process is to form algebraic equations which express relationships between the entries in the table and then to derive a solution from the equations.

The same basic approach can be used to model a problem on a spreadsheet. A table describing the problem is entered into the spreadsheet, the relationships between the variables and the constants becoming the spreadsheet formulas. Solutions are determined by varying the values of the variables until the correct answer is found. Although not a substitute for a complete algebraic solution, the spreadsheet approach is valuable because it helps in setting up word problems and testing the correctness of potential solutions, gives insight into the effects of changes of variables, and provides an introduction to modeling and trial-and-error solution techniques.

The spreadsheet implementation (Figure 26-1) illustrates a standard rate problem.

Example: Joan paddles a canoe at the rate of 5 miles per hour. During a river trip she took 3 hours going downstream and 8 hours returning. What was the speed of the current? How long was Joan's trip? How fast must Joan paddle to complete the same trip in 10 hours? In 9 hours?

In using the spreadsheet, an estimate of the current's speed is entered into cell B4. This estimate can be adjusted continually until the distances traveled in each direction (D5 and D6) are identical, as shown in the sample output. The current speed and the distance traveled are then given in cells B4 and D5, respectively. These values are used in the lower portion of the spreadsheet to calculate the effect that adjustments in Joan's paddling rate will have on the time for the trip.

For example, the output shows that Joan's trip is 21.8181 miles, that the speed of the current is 2.2727 miles per hour, and that by increasing her speed to 5.2 miles per hour, Joan can reduce the time for the trip to 10.37 hours.

SPREADSHEET CONSTRUCTION

Enter the data (cells B3, C5, and C6) and the formulas as indicated. Cells B4 and B11 are used to enter estimates for unknown quantities. Formulas in the lower portion use the values for river speed (B4) and distance (D5 and D6) obtained experimentally in the upper half.

Output

	A	B	C	D
1	1. FIND RIVER SPEED (B4)			
2		RATE	TIME	DISTANCE
3	JOAN	5		
4	RIVER	2.2727		
5	NET DOWN	7.2727	3	21.8181
6	NET UP	2.7273	8	21.8181
7		TOT HRS=	11	
8				
9	2. VARY JOAN'S RATE (B11)			
10		RATE	TIME	DISTANCE
11	JOAN	5.2		
12	RIVER	2.2727		
13	NET DOWN	7.4727	2.919708	21.8181
14	NET UP	2.9273	7.453421	21.8181
15		TOT HRS=	10.37313	

Formulas (R)

	A	B	C	D
1	1. FIND R	IVER SPEE	D (B4)	
2		RATE	TIME	DISTANCE
3	JOAN	5		
4	RIVER	2.2727		
5	NET DOWN	+B3+B4	3	+B5*C5
6	NET UP	+B3-B4	8	+B6*C6
7		TOT HRS=	+C5+C6	
8				
9	2. VARY J	OAN'S RAT	E (B11)	
10		RATE	TIME	DISTANCE
11	JOAN	5.2		
12	RIVER	+B4		
13	NET DOWN	+B11+B12	+D5/B13	+B13*C13
14	NET UP	+B11-B12	+D6/B14	+B14*C14
15		TOT HRS=	+C13+C14	

Figure 26-1 Algebraic word problems.

USER INTERACTION

1. Determine the speed of the current by modifying the value of cell B4 continually until the downstream and upstream distances (D5 and D6) are equal.

2. Vary the value of cell B11 to determine the effect of changing Joan's speed.

3. Modify the original parameters of the problem (cells B3, C5, and C6).

Exercises and Modifications

Design spreadsheets for the following algebra problems.

26-1. How much pure acid should be added to 8 liters of a 10% acid solution to obtain a 20% solution?

26-2. A blend is made from two varieties of coffee, one costing $2 per pound and the other costing $3.40 per pound. What proportions of the two varieties will result in a blend which costs $3 per pound [3]?

26-3. A 10-foot ladder leans against a wall; the bottom of the ladder is 5 feet from the wall. If the bottom is moved out an additional 2 feet, how far does the top of the ladder move down the wall?

Design spreadsheets for the following calculus max-min problems.

26-4. Find the dimensions of the most economical box having a square base and volume of 300 cubic inches which can be constructed using material for the bottom costing 4 cents per square inch and material for the top and sides costing 3 cents per square inch. Design the spreadsheet so that costs are parameters that can readily be changed.

26-5. If 30 pear trees are planted per acre, an orchard will produce 500 pears per tree. For each additional tree planted per acre the crop from each tree in the orchard decreases by 10 pears. How many trees per acre should be planted to maximize the output of the orchard?

REFERENCES

Algebra: references 19, 34, and 50.

Calculus: references 2, 43, 50, and 55.

Trigonometry
Indirect
Measurement

Spreadsheets can be useful both in solving trigonometry problems and in demonstrating the effect that errors in measurement can have upon calculated values.

Example: A woman on an offshore island estimates the angles α and β (in degrees) to an onshore lighthouse from two points x meters apart on the island. From these estimates, determine the distances B, C, and D in Figure 27-1.

It can be shown that the answers are

$$B = \frac{x \tan \beta}{\tan \alpha - \tan \beta} \qquad C = B \tan \alpha \qquad D = \sqrt{B^2 + C^2}$$

These values are calculated in the spreadsheet (Figure 27-2) using two similar sets of measurements. Note the great disparity in the answers caused by small variances in measurements. Further effects of measurement errors can be observed by modifying the data.

SPREADSHEET CONSTRUCTION

Enter the data into cells ‖B1 to C3‖ and the factor for converting from degrees to radians (@PI/180) into cell B4. Enter the formulas as shown.

USER INTERACTION

Vary the measurements for x (cells B1 and C1), α (cells B2 and C2), and β (cells B3 and C3).

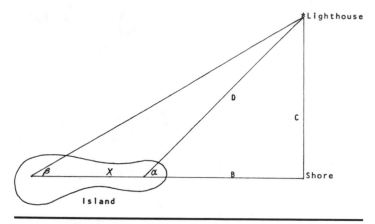

Figure 27-1 Estimating distances.

Exercises and Modifications

Create spreadsheets for the following problems. Illustrate the effects that will be caused by errors in measurement.

27-1. From a tower 1400 feet high a pizza shop is seen with an angle of depression of 10°. How far is it from the base of the tower to the pizza shop?

27-2. A kite makes an angle of 50° with the ground when 123 feet of line is out. How high is the kite?

27-3. A guy wire to the top of a pole makes a 67° angle with the ground. From a point 32 feet farther from the pole than the wire the angle of elevation of the top of the pole is 38°. How long is the wire? How tall is the pole?

```
                  Output                        Formulas (R)

           A        B       C           A         B       C
   |-------------|-------|-------|-  |-----------|--------|---|-
 1 | X(METERS)=     50      50     1 | X(METERS)=  50       50
 2 |    ALPHA=      27      28     2 | ALPHA=      27       28
 3 |     BETA=      26      25     3 | BETA=       26       25
 4 | DEG-TO-RAD:  .01745           4 | DEG-TO-RAD: @PI/180
 5 |                               5 |
 6 | TO LAND(B): 1119.02  356.49   6 | TO LAND(B): <B6>    <C6>
 7 |    DIST(C):  570.17  189.55   7 | DIST(C):    <B7>    <C7>
 8 | HYPOT(D):   1255.90  403.76   8 | HYPOT(D):   <B8>    <C8>

    B6: +B1*@TAN(B4*B3)/(@TAN(B4*B2)-@TAN(B4*B3))
    C6: +C1*@TAN(B4*C3)/(@TAN(B4*C2)-@TAN(B4*C3))
    B7: +B6*@TAN(B4*B2)        C7:  +C6*@TAN(B4*C2)
    B8: @SQRT((B6*B6)+(B7*B7)) C8:  @SQRT((C6*C6)+(C7*C7))
```

Figure 27-2 Indirect measurement by trigonometry.

27-4. Two airplanes leave an airport at noon. The first flies north-northwest at 250 miles per hour. The second flies due west at 200 miles per hour. How far apart are the planes at 12:45 p.m.? At 1 p.m.?

27-5. Design spreadsheets to investigate various identities, for example,

$$\sin (a + b) = \sin a \cos b + \cos a \sin b$$

$$\sin x = \cos \left(\frac{\pi}{2} - x\right)$$

REFERENCES

Trigonometry: references 20 and 34.

Compound Interest

If a given principal p is deposited at a compound interest rate r (for example, 8% corresponds to $r = 0.08$) compounded n times a year, its value $P(t)$ after t years is given by:

$$P(t) = p \left(1 + \frac{r}{n}\right)^{nt}$$

This example compares the growth of a given principle at two different rates of interest. Similar examples of exponential growth (or decay) arise in modeling population growth and related processes, as well as in a variety of business settings. The spreadsheet is shown in Figure 28-1.

SPREADSHEET CONSTRUCTION

1. Enter the principal into cell B3, the frequency of compounding into cell B4, two interest rates into cells B7 and C7, and selected years into column A.

2. Row 9 is used to display the initial principal. Enter +B3 into cells B9 and C9.

3. The value of the principal p at rate r after t years if interest is compounded n times a year is $p(1 + r/n)^{nt}$. Enter

    +B3*((1+(B7/B4))^(A10*B4))   and   +B3*((1+(C7/B4))^(A10*B4))

    into cells B10 and C10 and replicate (columns B and C).

USER INTERACTION

1. Vary the initial principal (B3) or the number of compounding periods per year (B4).

2. Vary the two rates being compared (cells B7 and C7).

3. Change the number of years in the table (cells A9 to A19).

Exercises and Modifications

28-1. Modify the spreadsheet by adding more columns to allow several interest rates to be compared.

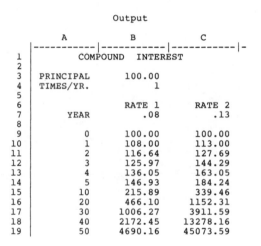

```
                         Output

               A          B            C
    |----------|------------|------------|-
 1  |         COMPOUND   INTEREST
 2  |
 3  | PRINCIPAL      100.00
 4  | TIMES/YR.           1
 5  |
 6  |              RATE 1       RATE 2
 7  | YEAR            .08          .13
 8  |
 9  |      0       100.00       100.00
10  |      1       108.00       113.00
11  |      2       116.64       127.69
12  |      3       125.97       144.29
13  |      4       136.05       163.05
14  |      5       146.93       184.24
15  |     10       215.89       339.46
16  |     20       466.10      1152.31
17  |     30      1006.27      3911.59
18  |     40      2172.45     13278.16
19  |     50      4690.16     45073.59
```

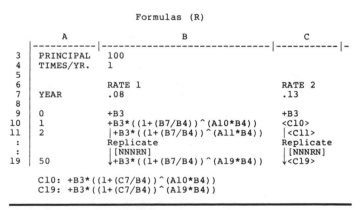

```
                      Formulas (R)

         A                          B                        C
    |----------|-----------------------------------|-----------|-
 3  | PRINCIPAL    100
 4  | TIMES/YR.    1
 5  |
 6  |              RATE 1                              RATE 2
 7  | YEAR         .08                                 .13
 8  |
 9  |  0           +B3                                 +B3
10  |  1           +B3*((1+(B7/B4))^(A10*B4))          <C10>
11  |  2          |+B3*((1+(B7/B4))^(A11*B4))         |<C11>
 :  |             Replicate                           Replicate
 :  |             |[NNNRN]                            |[NNNRN]
19  |  50         ↓+B3*((1+(B7/B4))^(A19*B4))         ↓<C19>

       C10:  +B3*((1+(C7/B4))^(A10*B4))
       C19:  +B3*((1+(C7/B4))^(A19*B4))
```

Figure 28-1 Compound interest.

28-2. Interchange the roles of times per year and the interest rate so that the effect of compounding at different frequencies can be compared.

28-3. Modify the spreadsheet to project the population growth of two countries using data from a current almanac, e.g., the United States (population 227 million, growth rate 0.7%) and Mexico (population 70 million, growth rate 3.3%).

28-4. Design a spreadsheet in which each period's principal is calculated iteratively; e.g., annual interest at 8% is defined by $p_{n+1} = 1.08p_n$. Modify column A to act as a counter.

28-5. Modify the spreadsheets in this section to include regular deposits or withdrawals. Construct spreadsheets for home mortgage payments, installment payments, or annuities.

REFERENCES

Financial mathematics and interest: references 18, 20, 27, 40, 42, 50, and 63.

Business applications of spreadsheets: references 13, 15, 56, and 57.

Population: reference 18.

29

Personal
Finance Model

The electronic spreadsheet was designed primarily for use with business and financial models. This demonstration illustrates such an application through a personal finance example.

Example: Suppose a person wants to make a budget projection for the coming year by constructing a model based on the following assumptions:

- Monthly income will start at $1500 and increase by 10% in April.
- The rate of inflation will be 1% per month throughout the year.
- A savings account will pay 6% interest compounded monthly.
- Food and automobile expenses will vary with the inflation rate.
- Mortgage expense will be constant; insurance payments will vary.
- Some income will be set aside for contributions (10%) and investment (5%).
- The initial savings account balance will be $1000; surpluses will go into the account and deficits will be made up from it.

The spreadsheet (Figure 29-1) incorporates these assumptions and generates a display similar to one worked by hand. Only a few numbers are entered directly into the spreadsheet since most cells receive their values by referring to values in other cells. For example, the food expense for March (D6) is the product, +D4*C6, of the current inflation rate (D4) and the food expense for the previous month (C6), while April's income (E2), 1.1*D2, is 10% above March's. Most of the spreadsheet can be completed using replication.

The spreadsheet makes it easy to see the effect of any modifications of the assumptions. For example, if the initial income (B2) is reduced to

$1400, the value of cell B10 becomes 140, the value of cell E2 becomes 1540, etc. Such a reduction in pay could be offset by various other reductions, each of which can be investigated using the spreadsheet.

SPREADSHEET CONSTRUCTION

1. Enter the constants into column B, the sporadic insurance payments into row 11, and the initial savings balance (1000) into cell A15.

2. Enter the basic formulas into columns B and C. For example, the value of the savings account in January (cell B15) is the sum of the previous balance (A15) multiplied by the interest factor (B3) plus the net difference between monthly income (B2) and expenses (B13), that is, +B3*A15+B2−B13.

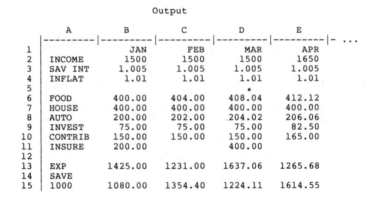

```
                                Output

          A          B          C          D          E
      |---------|----------|----------|----------|----------|- ...
  1              JAN        FEB        MAR        APR
  2   INCOME     1500       1500       1500       1650
  3   SAV INT    1.005      1.005      1.005      1.005
  4   INFLAT     1.01       1.01       1.01       1.01
  5                                     *
  6   FOOD       400.00     404.00     408.04     412.12
  7   HOUSE      400.00     400.00     400.00     400.00
  8   AUTO       200.00     202.00     204.02     206.06
  9   INVEST     75.00      75.00      75.00      82.50
 10   CONTRIB    150.00     150.00     150.00     165.00
 11   INSURE     200.00                400.00
 12
 13   EXP        1425.00    1231.00    1637.06    1265.68
 14   SAVE
 15   1000       1080.00    1354.40    1224.11    1614.55


                              Formulas (C)

          A            B              C              D              E
      |--------|---------------|---------------|---------------|------------|-
  1            JAN             FEB             MAR             APR
  2   INCOME   1500            +B2             +C2             1.1*D2
  3   SAV INT  1.005           +B3             +C3             +D3
  4   INFLAT   1.01            +B4             +C4             +D4
  5
  6   FOOD     400             +C4*B6          +D4*C6          +E4*D6
  7   HOUSE    400             +B7             +C7             +D7
  8   AUTO     200             +C4*B8          +D4*C8          +E4*D8
  9   INVEST   .05*B2          .05*C2          .05*D2          .05*E2
 10   CONTRIB  .1*B2           .1*C2           .1*D2           .1*E2
 11   INSURE   200                             400
 12
 13   EXP      @SUM(B6...B11)  @SUM(C6...C11)  @SUM(D6...D11)  @SUM(E6...E11)
 14   SAVE
 15   1000     +B3*A15+B2-B13  +C3*B15+C2-C13  +D3*C15+D2-D13  +E3*D15+E2-E13

      Replicate across rows [all R]
```

Figure 29-1 The personal finance model.

3. Replicate all formulas across rows with all locations relative. Note that if the inflation rate, for example, is decreased to 0.5% in March, changing the entry in cell D4 to 1.005 will mean that the remaining cells in row 4 show the value of 1.005.

4. Enter the formula 1.1*D2 into cell E2 to generate a 10% pay raise beginning in April.

USER INTERACTION

Vary any of the basic assumptions.

Exercises and Modifications

29-1. Modify the spreadsheet by adding other expenses, say clothing, or additional income, say investments.

29-2. Design your own personal finance model. Create a spreadsheet model for a school, business, church, or other institution.

29-3. Construct a checking account model.

29-4. Create a 1040 Income Tax form, complete with state sales and income tax tables (use the @LOOKUP function).

REFERENCES

Business or financial spreadsheet examples: references 13, 15, 56, and 57.

30

Linear Programming (Simplex) with User-Selected Pivots

Linear programming is a relatively new branch of mathematics, with applications in such diverse areas as economics, engineering, agriculture, sociology, nutrition, business, and national defense. Linear programming considers problems of optimizing linear functions subject to linear constraints. The primary tool used in solving such problems is the simplex algorithm, which is based on the pivot method (gaussian elimination) for solving systems of linear equations. The algorithm is too lengthy to present in full here. A complete discussion can be found in Ref. 54.

In this demonstration the spreadsheet designed to solve a linear program requires user interaction in choosing pivot locations at each stage of the algorithm. This makes the spreadsheet useful for studying the operation of the simplex algorithm. Demonstration 31 presents a more complex spreadsheet in which the program selects the pivot locations. Both will be illustrated by the same example.

Example: A farmer wishes to produce two crops using the following resources: 100 acres of land, 160 worker-hours of labor, and $1100 of capital. Each crop requires the expenditure of some of the resources and has an expected profit, given by

	Crop I	Crop II
Area planted, acres	x_1	x_2
Labor required, worker-hours per acre	1	4
Capital required, per acre	$10	$20
Expected profit, per acre	$30	$100

How much of each crop should be planted to maximize expected profit?

The problem is modeled by the following linear program:

Maximize: $P(x_1, x_2) = 30x_1 + 100x_2$ profit
Subject to: $x_1 + x_2 \leq 100$ land constraint
$x_1 + 4x_2 \leq 160$ labor constraint
$10x_1 + 20x_2 \leq 1100$ capital constraint
$x_1, x_2 \geq 0$

The spreadsheet implementation is shown in Figure 30-1. The format, including slack variables, is consistent with that used in most linear programming texts. (Although some texts use the negative of the objective function, the same spreadsheet can be used; see Exercise 30-6). The following is a brief guide to the interaction required of the user; for details, consult Refs. 40, 50, or 54, among others.

Step 0
a. Write each constraint inequality as an equation by introducing nonnegative slack variables

$$x_1 + x_2 + s_1 = 100$$
$$x_1 + 4x_2 + s_2 = 160$$
$$10x_1 + 20x_2 + s_3 = 1100$$

Enter the coefficients into the spreadsheet as indicated.
b. Enter the coefficients of the objective (profit) function:

$$P = 30x_1 + 100x_2 + 0s_1 + 0s_2 + 0s_3 + 0$$

Step 1 (refer to rows 6 to 9)
a. Any column for a variable (labeled 1, 2, 3, 4, 5) that has a positive entry in the objective row (row 9) may serve as the pivot column. Both columns 1 and 2 have positive entries (30 and 100). Generally, choosing the column with the largest entry is the most efficient choice. Enter 2 into cell B11.
b. The program now divides the column of constants (column G) by the entries in the pivot column, to produce column H. The pivot equation selected must be the row with the smallest positive

entry in column H. For the first, second, or third equation enter 1, 2, or 3, respectively. Since the smallest positive entry, 40, occurs in the second equation, enter 2 into cell B12.

c. A gaussian pivot is performed by the program, pivoting on the entry in variable 2 in the second equation. The resulting matrix appears in rows 16 to 19. The new basic solution is $x_1 = 0$, $x_2 = 40$, $s_1 = 60$, $s_2 = 0$, $s_3 = 300$. The value of the objective function at this point is 4000, the negative of the entry in cell G19.

Step 2 Repeat step 1 on the new matrix in rows 16 to 19

a. The only positive entry in the new objective row (row 19) is 5, in the column of variable 1. Enter 1 into cell B21.

b. The smallest positive entry in column H is 60, which occurs in the third equation. Enter 3 into cell B22.

c. After the pivot has been performed, the resulting matrix appears in rows 26 to 29. Since there are no positive entries in the next objective row (row 29), the algorithm has arrived at the optimal solution

$$\text{Crop I } x_1 = 60$$

$$\text{Crop II } x_2 = 25$$

Output

	A	B	C	D	E	F	G	H
4	VAR->	1	2	3	4	5		
5		CROP1	CROP2	S1	S2	S3	CON	
6	LAND	1	1	1	0	0	100	100
7	LABOR	1	4	0	1	0	160	40
8	CAP ($)	10	20	0	0	1	1100	55
9	PROFIT	30	100	0	0	0	0	
10	SELECT							
11	VAR:	2		1	<COL	2		
12	EQ:	2		4				
13				20				
14				100				
15								
16	1	.75	0	1	-.25	0	60	80
17	2	.25	1	0	.25	0	40	160
18	3	5	0	0	-5	1	300	60
19	OB:	5	0	0	-25	0	-4000	
20	SELECT							
21	VAR:	1		.75	<COL	1		
22	EQ:	3		.25				
23				5				
24				5				
25								
26	1	0	0	1	.5	-.15	15	NA
27	2	0	1	0	.5	-.05	25	NA
28	3	1	0	0	-1	.2	60	NA
29	OB:	0	0	0	-20	-1	-4300	

Figure 30-1 Simplex linear programming with user-selected pivots.

Slack Land $s_1 = 15$

Slack Labor $s_2 = 0$

Slack Capital $s_3 = 0$

Maximum Profit $P = \$4300$

```
                            Formulas (R)

       A        B        C        D      E      F       G            H
   |--------|-------|-------|------|-----|-----|------|------------|-
 4 | VAR->    1        2        3      4      5
 5 |          CROP1    CROP2    S1     S2     S3    CON
 6 | LAND     1        1        1      0      0     100     <H6>
 7 | LABOR    1        4        0      1      0     160    |<H7>
                                                           Rep.[NRRRRRRRRRR]
 8 | CAP($)   10       20       0      0      1     1100   ↓<H8>
 9 | PROFIT   30       100      0      0      0     0
10 | SELECT
11 | VAR:     2                 <D11>  <COL  +B11
12 | EQ:      2                |<D12>
                               Rep.[NRRRRR]
13 |                          |<D13>
14 |                          ↓<D14>
15 |
                 ---Replicate: N,RN,RRNN,RRNN--->
16 | 1        <B16>   <C16>   <D16>   <E16> <F16> <G16>   <H16>
                 ---Replicate: N,RRNN,RN,RRNN--->          |
17 | 2        <B17>   <C17>   <D17>   <E17> <F17> <G17>   |<H17>
                 ---Replicate: N,RRNN,RRNN,RN--->
18 | 3        <B18>   <C18>   <D18>   <E18> <F18> <G18>   ↓<H18>
                 ---Replicate: N,RRNN,RRNN,RRNN->          Replicate
19 | OB:      <B19>   <C19>   <D19>   <E19> <F19> <G19>   [NRRRRRRRRRR]
```

Replicate rows 10-19 into rows 20-29, 30-39, ... : all variables
relative

H6 : @CHOOSE(B11,G6/B6,G6/C6,G6/D6,G6/E6,G6/F6)
...
H8 : @CHOOSE(B11,G8/B8,G8/C8,G8/D8,G8/E8,G8/F8)

D11: @CHOOSE(B11,B6,C6,D6,E6,F6)   D12: @CHOOSE(B11,B7,C7,D7,E7,F7)
D13: @CHOOSE(B11,B8,C8,D8,E8,F8)   D14: @CHOOSE(B11,B9,C9,D9,E9,F9)

B16: @CHOOSE(B12,B6/D11,B6-(B7/D12*D11),B6-(B8/D13*D11))
...
G16: @CHOOSE(B12,G6/D11,G6-(G7/D12*D11),G6-(G8/D13*D11))

B17: @CHOOSE(B12,B7-(B6/D11*D12),B7/D12,B7-(B8/D13*D12))
...
G17: @CHOOSE(B12,G7-(G6/D11*D12),G7/D12,G7-(G8/D13*D12))

B18: @CHOOSE(B12,B8-(B6/D11*D13),B8-(B7/D12*D13),B8/D13)
...
G18: @CHOOSE(B12,G8-(G6/D11*D13),G8-(G7/D12*D13),G8/D13)

B19: @CHOOSE(B12,B9-(B6/D11*D14),B9-(B7/D12*D14),B9-(B8/D13*D14))
...
G19: @CHOOSE(B12,G9-(G6/D11*D14),G9-(G7/D12*D14),G9-(G8/D13*D14))

H16: @CHOOSE(B21,G16/B16,G16/C16,G16/D16,G16/E16,G16/F16)
...
H18: @CHOOSE(B21,G18/B18,G18/C18,G18/D18,G18/E18,G18/F18)

Figure 30-1 *Continued.*

Steps 3, 4, 5 . . .

If the algorithm has not reached optimality after two steps, replicate rows 20 to 29 into rows 30 to 39, 40 to 49, . . . and repeat the process.

POSTOPTIMALITY ANALYSIS

1. At optimality the entries in the objective row beneath the slack variables are the negatives of the marginal values of the resources [40, p. 342; 54, pp. 159–162]: land (E29), $0 per acre; labor (F29), $20 per worker-hour; return on capital (G29), $1 per dollar.

2. If any of the original data are changed, the spreadsheet is recalculated. If the same variables are basic in the optimal solution [54], the new optimal solution can be read off from the final matrix. Otherwise, it is necessary to make alternate pivots in intermediate steps to obtain the optimal solution. The spreadsheet of Demonstration 31 eliminates the need for user-selected pivots.

SPREADSHEET CONSTRUCTION

1. Enter the constraint coefficients, constants, and objective function into rows 6 to 9, as shown.

2. Enter the rest of the expressions as shown in rows 6 to 19.

3. Replicate rows 10 to 19 into rows 20 to 29, 30 to 39, . . . , treating all locations as relative.

USER INTERACTION

1. Make alternate pivots where possible (B11 and B12, B21 and B22, . . .). In this example, the first pivot can also be made using the first variable. (If this is done with the given example, a third iteration is needed.)

2. Vary the amounts of resources available (cells G6, G7, and G8), constraint coefficients (cells ‖B6 to C8‖), and profit coefficients (cells B9 and C9).

Exercises and Modifications

30-1. Solve the following problem by the simplex method:

$$\text{Maximize } f(x, y) = 4x + 3y \text{ subject to}$$
$$3x + 2y \leq 6$$

$$x - y \leqslant 4$$

$$4x + 5y \leqslant 10$$

$$x, y \geqslant 0$$

30-2. Extend the number of iterations in the spreadsheet.

30-3. Solve the following problem using the simplex method. A factory makes two products, X and Y. Each week the company has available 220 hours of lathe time, 120 hours of sanding time, and 160 hours of painting time. The time requirements in hours for each product are

	X	Y
Lathe	3	1.5
Sanding	1	2.5
Painting	4	2.0

The profit is $110 on each item of X and $65 on each item of Y. How many of each should be produced each week for the company to maximize its profit? What is the answer if the profit on each item of Y is reduced to $55?

30-4. Modify the spreadsheet to accommodate more unknowns and more (or fewer) constraints.

30-5. See Demonstration 31 for exercises concerning postoptimality analysis.

30-6. Modify row 9 of the spreadsheet so that the entries are the negatives of the coefficients of the objective function. Now carry out the simplex algorithm by pivoting on columns with negative entries in the objective rows. This is the format adopted in some linear programming books, e.g., Refs., 40, 50, and 54.

REFERENCES

Linear programming (simplex algorithm and applications): references 1, 10, 14, 27, 35, 36, 40, 48, 50, 54, and 63.   .

Postoptimality analysis: reference 54.

Linear Programming (Simplex) with Program-Selected Pivots

In Demonstration 30 the simplex algorithm for solving a linear program the spreadsheet format required user interaction in intermediate steps. The same algorithm and example are employed in the spreadsheet in Figures 31-1 to 31-3, but in this case no user involvement is required after the data have been entered. The data are entered into the top half of a split-screen display, and the solution is displayed in the bottom half. The display of pertinent rows and columns for a simplex linear programming problem is called a *tableau*.

This spreadsheet is explicitly designed for two variables, at most three constraints, and at most three iterations of the pivoting process. Increasing the number of any of these requires significant modifications in the spreadsheet. This is one example in which the spreadsheet design itself is very complex. It has been included as a dramatic illustration of the interactive features of a spreadsheet. Although only two pivots are needed for the selected example, some similar problems require three.

The spreadsheet uses the example of Demonstration 30:

$$\text{Maximize:} \quad P(x_1, x_2) = 30x_1 + 100x_2 \quad \text{profit}$$
$$\text{Subject to:} \quad x_1 + x_2 \leq 100 \quad \text{land constraint}$$
$$x_1 + 4x_2 \leq 160 \quad \text{labor constraint}$$

$$10x_1 + 20x_2 \leq 1100 \qquad \text{capital constraint}$$
$$x_1, x_2 \geq 0$$

The following steps describe the use of the spreadsheet once it has been constructed (note the use of the split screen).

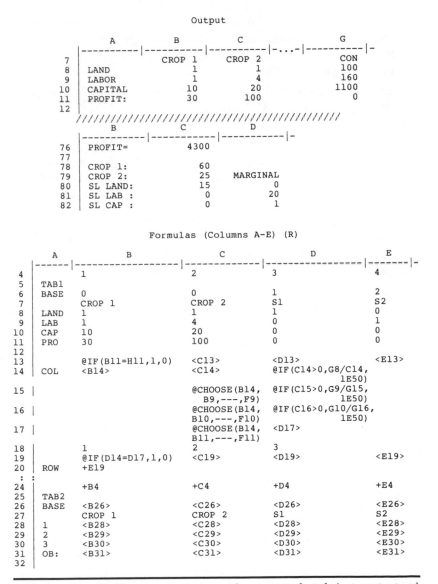

```
                              Output

            A            B            C                    G
      |----------|-----------|-----------|-...-|-----------|-
   7                      CROP 1      CROP 2                  CON
   8     LAND              1           1                      100
   9     LABOR             1           4                      160
  10     CAPITAL          10          20                     1100
  11     PROFIT:          30         100                        0
  12
          /////////////////////////////////////////////////
                   B            C            D
          |-----------|------------|------------|-
  76        PROFIT=        4300
  77
  78        CROP 1:          60
  79        CROP 2:          25       MARGINAL
  80        SL LAND:         15           0
  81        SL LAB :          0          20
  82        SL CAP :          0           1


                    Formulas (Columns A-E) (R)

        A            B                  C                  D              E
    |------|-------------------|--------------|-------------------|-------|-
   4              1                 2                 3              4
   5    TAB1
   6    BASE     0                 0                 1              2
   7              CROP 1            CROP 2            S1             S2
   8    LAND     1                 1                 1              0
   9    LAB      1                 4                 0              1
  10    CAP     10                20                 0              0
  11    PRO     30               100                 0              0
  12
  13           @IF(B11=H11,1,0)  <C13>             <D13>          <E13>
  14    COL    <B14>             <C14>             @IF(C14>0,G8/C14,
                                                        1E50)
  15   |                        @CHOOSE(B14,      @IF(C15>0,G9/G15,
                                   B9,---,F9)           1E50)
  16   |                        @CHOOSE(B14,      @IF(C16>0,G10/G16,
                                   B10,---,F10)          1E50)
  17   |                        @CHOOSE(B14,      <D17>
                                   B11,---,F11)
  18              1                 2                 3
  19           @IF(D14=D17,1,0)  <C19>             <D19>          <E19>
  20    ROW    +E19
   :  :
  24            +B4               +C4               +D4            +E4
  25    TAB2
  26    BASE   <B26>             <C26>             <D26>          <E26>
  27              CROP 1            CROP 2            S1             S2
  28     1      <B28>             <C28>             <D28>          <E28>
  29     2      <B29>             <C29>             <D29>          <E29>
  30     3      <B30>             <C30>             <D30>          <E30>
  31    OB:     <B31>             <C31>             <D31>          <E31>
  32
```

Figure 31-1 Simplex linear programming with program-selected pivots: output and formulas (columns A to E) [R].

Step 1 Enter the constraint and objective-function coefficients and constants as indicated into rows 8 to 11. The constraint constants (G8 to G10) must be nonnegative.

Step 2 Read off the answer from rows 76 to 82. The maximum profit is $4300, which results from planting 60 acres of crop I, 25 acres of crop II, with 15 acres of slack land, and no slack labor or capital. In addition, the marginal values of an acre of land, a worker-hour of labor, and a dollar of capital are $0, $20, and $1, respectively. (If a problem has no feasible solution, NA will be displayed.)

Step 3 Perform postoptimal analysis by varying any of the original data (see Exercises 31-1 and 31-2).

SPREADSHEET CONSTRUCTION

This is an extremely complex spreadsheet. Instead of discussing details at length, only a broad outline is given below. The courageous reader is encouraged to dig through the details in Figures 31-1 to 31-3.

1. Enter the constraint equations (including slack variables) and objective functions into rows 8 to 11, as shown.

2. Enter the remainder of the expressions in rows 1 to 32, as indicated. The second tableau is generated in rows 13 to 32.

```
           Formulas  (Columns  F-H)  (R)

             F        G              H
        |------|--------|------------------|-
     4  | 5
     5  |
     6  | 3
     7  | S3       CON
     8  | 0        100
     9  | 0        160
    10  | 1        1100
    11  | 0        0          @MAX(B11...F11)
    12  |
    13  | <F13>
     :  | no entries in rows 14-23
    24  | +F4
    25  |
    26  | <F26>
    27  | S3       CON
    28  | <F28>    <G28>
    29  | <F29>    <G29>
    30  | <F30>    <G30>
    31  | <F31>    <G31>      @MAX(B31...F31)
```

Figure 31-2 Simplex linear programming with program-selected pivots: formulas (columns F to H) [R]. Replicate rows 13 to 32 into rows 33 to 52, then into rows 53 to 72, treating all locations as relative.

3. Replicate rows 13 to 32 into rows 33 to 52 and then into rows 53 to 72 (with all locations relative) to obtain subsequent tableaux. If only two pivots are required, the construction of rows 53 to 72 can be omitted and the row coordinates of the cell references in rows 76 to 82 reduced by 20 each; i.e., in formulas, replace D71 with D51, B69 with B49, etc.

USER INTERACTION

Vary the amounts of resources (cells G8, G9, and G10), the constraint coefficients (cells ‖B8 to C10‖), and the profit coefficients (B11 and C11).

```
        Formulas (Rows 76-82)

            B    |     C     |     D
    |------------|-----------|-----------|-
 76 | PROFIT=        -G71
 77 |
 78 | CROP 1:        <C78>
 79 | CROP 2:        <C79>      MARGINAL
 80 | S LAND         <C80>       -D71
 81 | S LAB          <C81>       -E71
 82 | S CAP          <C82>       -F71
```

```
C13:  @IF(@MAX(B13...B13)=1,0,@IF(C11=H11,1,0))
      Replicate C13:D13...F13 [NRRN]
B14:  (B4*B13)+(C4*C13)+(D4*D13)+(E4*E13)+(F4*F13)
C14:  @CHOOSE(B14,B8,C8,D8,E8,F8)
D17:  @IF(@MIN(D14...D16)=1E50,@NA,@MIN(D14...D16))
C19:  @IF(B19=1,0,@IF(D15=D17,1,0))
D19:  @IF(@MAX(B19,C19)=1,0,@IF(D16=D17,1,0))
E19:  (B18*B19)+(C18*C19)+(D18*D19)


B26:  @IF(B14=B24,B20,@IF(B20=B6,0,B6))
C26:  @IF(B14=C24,B20,@IF(B20=C6,0,C6))
   :
F26:  @IF(B14=F24,B20,@IF(B20=F6,0,F6))


B28:  @CHOOSE(B20,B8/C14,B8-(B9/C15*C14),B8-(B10/C16*C14))
      Replicate B28: C28...G28 [NRNRRNNRRNN]
B29:  @CHOOSE(B20,B9-(B8/C14*C15),B9/C15,B9-(B10/C16*C15))
      Replicate B29: C29...G29 [NRNRNNRNRRNN]
B30:  @CHOOSE(B20,B10-(B8/C14*C16),B10-(B9/C15*C16),B10/C16)
      Replicate B30: C30...G30 [NRRNNRRNNRN]
B31:  @CHOOSE(B20,B11-(B8/C14*C17),B11-(B9/C15*C17),
                                B11-(B10/C16*C17))
      Replicate B31: C31...G31 [NRRNNRRNNRRNN]

C78:  @IF(B66=0,0,(B68*G68)+(B69*G69)+(B70*G70))
C79:  @IF(C66=0,0,(C68*G68)+(C69*G69)+(C70*G70))
C80:  @IF(D66=0,0,(D68*G68)+(D69*G69)+(D70*G70))
C81:  @IF(E66=0,0,(E68*G68)+(E69*G69)+(E70*G70))
C82:  @IF(F66=0,0,(F68*G68)+(F69*G69)+(F70*G70))
```

Figure 31-3 Simplex linear programming with program-selected pivots: formulas (rows 76 to 82). Replicate rows 13 to 32 into rows 33 to 52, then into rows 53 to 72, treating all locations as relative.

Exercises and Modifications

31-1. One at a time, increase the amount of available land, labor, and capital by 1 unit each and note that profit is increased by the marginal amount. Repeat, increasing each by 10 units. Repeat again, decreasing the available land to 50 acres.

31-2. Vary the parameters of the original model and observe the resulting changes at optimality. For example, what is the result of a drop to $40 in the expected profit of crop II? Of increasing the labor requirements of crop I to 2 worker-hours per acre?

31-3. Maximize each of the following functions over the region determined by the constraints: $4x + 5y \leq 20$, $9x + 4y \leq 36$, $x + 4y \leq 12$, $x \geq 0$, $y \geq 0$:
a. $f = x + 2y$ c. $f = x + 10y$
b. $f = 2x + y$ d. $f = 10x + y$

31-4. It is easy to modify the spreadsheet for fewer than three constraints; simply use $0x + 0y \leq 0$ for a missing constraint. Using this observation, solve the following linear program: maximize $3x + 6y$ subject to $3x + y \leq 60$, $x + 3y \leq 60$, $x, y \geq 0$.

31-5. A farmer plans to stock her farm pond with two species A and B of bass. The pond produces three foods (P, Q, and R) required by the bass. It produces 1000 units of P, 1400 units of Q, and 800 units of R per day. Species A requires 1, 2, and 3 units of these foods each day, and species B requires 3, 10, and 2. If the average weight of variety A is 12 ounces per fish and that of variety B is 20 ounces per fish, make the (unrealistic) assumption of steady state and determine how the farmer should stock her pond so that it will support the maximum total weight of the two varieties.

31-6. Modify the spreadsheet as in Exercise 30-6.

REFERENCES

Linear programming: references 1, 10, 14, 35, 36, 40, 48, 50, 54, and 63.

Game Theory

Game theory, which involves the study of competitive situations, has found application in models used in economics, engineering, and military and behavioral science, among others. This demonstration provides a spreadsheet implementation of a two-person zero-sum game. The discussion covers only a brief résumé of some results from game theory. For a development of the theory, complete statements of definitions, and a collection of applications, see Refs. 27, 40, and 49.

Consider the game described by the following 2×2 matrix, where the payoffs shown are to the row player, player 1:

	Player 2	
	Option I	Option II
Player 1		
Option I	$5	−$1
Option II	−$3	$4

Thus, if both players select their first options, player 1 wins $5 from player 2; if player 1 selects his option II and player 2 selects her option I, player 2 wins $3 from player 1, etc.

In game theory the object for each player is to develop an optimal strategy by choosing between the options in a random manner, but with fixed probabilities, so as to maximize the long-term expected payoff, i.e., to maximize expected winnings or to minimize expected losses if the game is unfavorable. It can be shown that the spreadsheet in Figure 32-1 accomplishes this for a game defined by any 2×2 matrix:

$$A = \begin{bmatrix} a & b \\ c & d \end{bmatrix}$$

Output

```
        A       B     C     D       E       F
   |-------|-------|-|-------|-------|-------|-
 1 | GAME THEORY: PAYOFFS ARE TO PLAYER 1
 2 |
 3 | POSSIBLE               PLAYER 2
 4 | STRATEGIES          OPT 1   OPT 2
 5 |                      .7      .3
 6 | PLAYER 1        /  ------  ------
 7 |   OPT 1    .6   /    5      -1
 8 |   OPT 2    .4   /   -3       4
 9 |                /  ------  ------
10 |                        VALUE=    1.56
   ///////////////////////////////////////////
20 | OPTIMAL                PLAYER 2
21 | STRATEGIES          OPT 1   OPT 2
22 |                    .3846   .6154
23 | PLAYER 1        /  ------  ------
24 |   OPT 1  .5385  /    5      -1
25 |   OPT 2  .4615  /   -3       4
26 |                /  ------  ------
27 |                      GAME  VALUE=   1.308
```

Formulas (R)

```
        A       B       C       D               E               F
   |-------|-------|----|---------------|---------------|---------------|-
 3 | POSSIB  LE          PLAY           ER 2
 4 | STRATE  GIES        OPT 1          OPT 2
 5 |                      .7            1-D5
 6 | PLAYER  1      /    ------         ------
 7 |   OPT 1  .6    /     5             -1
 8 |   OPT 2  1-B7  /    -3              4
 9 |               /    ------         ------
10 |                                   VALUE=          <F10>
11 |
12 |   CHECK       /    ------         ------
13 |    FOR        /    +D7            +E7             @MIN(D7,E7)
14 |  SADDLE       /    +D8            +E8             @MIN(D8,E8)
15 |               /    ------         ------
16 |                    @MAX(D7,D8)    @MAX(E7,E8)     <F16>
17 |
18 | SADDLE  <B18>  ROW1: <D18>        COL1:           <F18>
19 |
20 | OPTIMA  L:
21 | STRATE  GIES        OPT 1          OPT 2
22 |                    <D22>          1-D22
23 | PLAYER  1      /    ------         ------
24 |   OPT 1 <B24>  /    +D7            +E7
25 |   OPT 2 1-B24  /    +D8            +E8
26 |               /    ------         ------
27 |                    GAME           VALUE=          <F27>
```

```
F10:  (B7*D5*D7)+(B7*E5*E7)+(B8*D5*D8)+(B8*E5*E8)
F16:  @IF(@MAX(F13,F14)=@MIN(D16,E16),1,0)
B18:  @IF(F16=0,@NA,@MAX(F13,F14))
D18:  @IF(F13<>B18,0,@IF(@OR(F13<>F14,(D7+E7)>=(D8+E8)),1,0)
F18:  @IF(D16<>B18,0,@IF(@OR(D16<>E16,(D7+D8)<=(E7+E8)),1,0)
D22:  @IF(F16=0,(E8-E7)/(D7+E8-E7-D8),F16*F18)
B24:  @IF(F16=0,(E8-D8)/(D7+E8-E7-D8),F16*D18)
F27:  (B24*D22*D7)+(B24*E22*E7)+(B25*D22*D8)+(B25*E22*E8)
```

Figure 32-1 Game theory.

The expected payoff to player 1 if both players use their optimal strate-gies is called the *value* of the game. The spreadsheet consists of three parts:

1. If player 1 plays his options I and II with probabilities $P(I)$ and $P(II)$ and player 2 plays her options I and II with probabilities $Q(I)$ and $Q(II)$, the expected value of the game (to player 1) is

$$E = 5P(I)Q(I) - 1P(I)Q(II) - 3P(II)Q(I) + 4P(II)Q(II)$$

The results of different choices of strategy by the two players can be investigated in rows 3 to 10. Player 1's choice for $P(I)$ is entered into cell B7 and player 2's $Q(I)$ into cell D5. Values for $P(II)$ and $Q(II)$ are then calculated in cells B8 and E5. The resulting expected value of the game for those strategies is shown in cell F10. For example, the sample output below shows that if $P(I) = .6$, $P(II) = .4$, $Q(I) = .7$, and $Q(II) = .3$, then the expected value for player 1 is \$1.56.

2. The game will have a saddle-point solution if the maximum of the row minimums is the same as the minimum of the column maxi-mums. This is determined in rows 12 to 18. If there is a saddle point, cell F16 is set to 1; otherwise it is set to 0. Cell B18 lists any saddle value. If there is a saddle point, each player's strategy will consist of choosing the same option each time, i.e., the row (column) of the saddle point, with ties resolved by row (column) dominance [49]. If the game has a saddle point, cell D18 determines whether row 1 is player 1's choice and cell F18 determines whether column 1 is player 2's choice.

3. Finally, rows 20 to 27 determine the optimal strategies. If there is no saddle point, the optimal strategies for a game determined by matrix A are

$$P(I) = \frac{d - c}{a - b - c + d} \quad \text{and} \quad Q(I) = \frac{d - b}{a - b - c + d}$$

The value of the game is

$$V = \frac{ad - bc}{a - b - c + d}$$

[46, 49]. The optimal strategies, whether there is a saddle-point solu-tion or not, are shown for player 1 in cells B24 and B25 and for player 2 in cells D22 and E22. The value of the game is displayed in cell F27. Note that the game illustrated in the example is favorable to player 1, with value \$1.31.

By instituting a window in the spreadsheet, as shown in the output (Figure 32-1), a user can enter a game into the upper half of the screen display, experiment with various strategies there, and observe the optimal strategies in the lower half.

USER INTERACTION

1. Change the payoff values (cells D7, E7, D8, and E8).
2. Vary the strategy of player 1 (cell B7) and player 2 (cell D5).

Exercises and Modifications

32-1. Assign to player 1 (in B7) the optimal strategy obtained from B24. Observe that for any strategy of player 2 (vary D5) the game has the same expected value. Thus, by playing his optimal strategy in the game above, player 1 ensures that his long-term winnings will average $1.31 per time regardless of what player 2 does.

32-2. Suppose that player 2 has chosen to use .3 as her strategy I (D5). By varying the value of B7 observe that player 1 can now do better than if player 2 had chosen her optimal strategy.

*32-3. Design a spreadsheet for a $2 \times n$ or an $n \times 2$ game for $n = 3$, 4, ...

Find and implement the matrices for the following games and observe the optimal strategies.

32-4. Players 1 and 2 each hold up either one or two fingers. If the numbers match, player 1 wins $1 from player 2; otherwise, player 2 wins $1 from player 1. Does one player have an advantage?

32-5. Players 1 and 2 hold up fingers as in Exercise 32-4. If the numbers match, player 1 wins from player 2 an amount in dollars equal to the sum of the fingers ($2 or $4); otherwise, player 2 wins from player 1 an amount in dollars equal to the sum of the fingers ($3). Does one player have an advantage?

32-6. John Gotrocks offers to spend the afternoon playing the following game with you. He will hide behind his back either a $10 bill or a $20 bill and will ask you to guess which it is. If you guess correctly, you get the money, otherwise you get nothing.

John expects to reward cleverness. What is your optimal strategy?

REFERENCES

Game theory and applications: references 6, 10, 27, 36, 46, 49, and 63.

Solution of 2 × 2 games: references 46 and 49.

Demonstrations of Circular Reference

Demonstrations 33 to 36 illustrate the use of circular and self-reference to create spreadsheet implementations of algorithms. In each demonstration a few cells are used repeatedly to carry out a series of computations. In Demonstrations 33, 34, and 36 the screen display is continually updated by the use of the recalculate command. Each spreadsheet program has its own conventions for circular reference and recalculation. A user's manual should be consulted for details.

Demonstration

33

Compact Spreadsheets

This demonstration contains examples of the use of circular reference and recalculation to create compact spreadsheets for algorithms examined in earlier sections.

33-1 FACTORIALS

Recall from Demonstration 2 that $n!$ is defined recursively by

$$1! = 1 \qquad n! = n(n-1)! \qquad \text{for } n > 1$$

In the spreadsheet in Figure 33-1 the values of n and $n!$ are calculated in cells A5 and B5. Cell A3 is used to initialize the spreadsheet. If the value of A3 is 0, the values of A5 and B5 become 0 and 1, respectively. When any nonzero number (say 1) is entered into cell A3 and each time the recalculation key is pressed thereafter, the value of A5 is increased by 1, and the previous value of B5 ($n!$) is multiplied by the updated value of A5, exactly as in the recurrence relation.

33-2 FIBONACCI NUMBERS

The Fibonacci numbers (Demonstration 1) are defined recursively by the relation

$$a_1 = 1, \, a_2 = 1, \, a_{n+2} = a_n + a_{n+1} \qquad \text{for } n > 0$$

In the spreadsheet in Figure 33-2 the values of a_1 and a_2 are entered as parameters into cells B5 and B6. Cell B3 is used to initialize the spreadsheet.

Demonstration 33 - Compact Spreadsheets (Factorials)

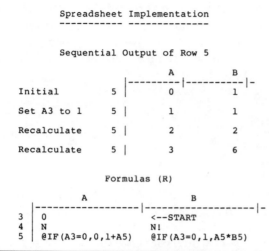

```
                    Spreadsheet Implementation
                    ----------- --------------


                    Sequential Output of Row 5

                                    A             B
                            |---------|----------|-
        Initial          5  |    0          1
        
        Set A3 to 1      5  |    1          1
        
        Recalculate      5  |    2          2
        
        Recalculate      5  |    3          6
        
        
                        Formulas (R)
        
                A                           B
        |-------------------|--------------------|-
     3  |  0                     <--START
     4  |  N                     N!
     5  |  @IF(A3=0,0,1+A5)      @IF(A3=0,1,A5*B5)
```

Figure 33-1 Compact spreadsheet for factorials.

Values for n, $n + 1$, and $n + 2$ are calculated in cells C4 to C6. As long as the value of cell B3 is 0, these values are 1, 2, and 3, respectively. When B3 is set to a nonzero value, say 1, and each time the recalculation key is pressed thereafter, the values of cells C4 to C6 are increased by 1.

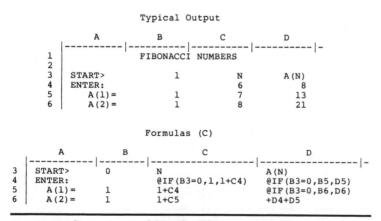

```
                        Typical Output

                A          B          C          D
        |----------|----------|----------|----------|-
     1  |               FIBONACCI  NUMBERS
     2  |
     3  |  START>         1          N        A(N)
     4  |  ENTER:                    6          8
     5  |    A(1)=        1          7         13
     6  |    A(2)=        1          8         21


                        Formulas (C)

            A        B              C                   D
    |-----------|--------|--------------------|------------------|-
  3 |  START>       0       N                    A(N)
  4 |  ENTER:               @IF(B3=0,1,1+C4)     @IF(B3=0,B5,D5)
  5 |    A(1)=      1       1+C4                  @IF(B3=0,B6,D6)
  6 |    A(2)=      1       1+C5                  +D4+D5
```

Figure 33-2 Compact spreadsheet for Fibonacci numbers.

The values of a_n, a_{n+1}, and a_{n+2} are calculated in cells D4 to D6. The entry in D6 is always the sum of the two previous numbers. As long as B3 is 0, the values in D4 and D5 are copied from B5 and B6. After B3 has changed to a nonzero value and each time the recalculation key is pressed thereafter, the previous value of D5 becomes the new value of D4, the previous value of D6 becomes the new value of D5, and the new value of D6 is the sum of D4 and D5.

33-3   BISECTION ALGORITHM

This example is developed for

$$f(x) = x^2 - 2$$

If a function is continuous on the interval $[a, b]$ and if $f(a)$ and $f(b)$ have opposite signs, that is, $f(a)f(b) < 0$, then f has a zero in $[a, b]$. The bisection algorithm uses this fact to generate a sequence of decreasing intervals $[a_i, b_i]$ the midpoints of which converge to the zero (see Demonstration 3). In the spreadsheet (Figure 33-3) an initial interval is entered into cells A5 and B5 and is copied into cells A6 and B6 while the entry in cell B3 is 0. The midpoint of interval [A6, B6] is computed in cell C6. Once B3 is set to a nonzero value, a new interval, either [A6, C6] or [C6, B6], is obtained with each recalculation and entered into cells A6 and B6.

```
                Sequential Output of Row 6

                         A         B         C
                 |---------|---------|---------|-
    Initial      6 |       1         2        1.5

    Set B3 to 1  6 |       1        1.5       1.25

    Recalculate  6 |     1.25       1.5      1.375

    Recalculate  6 |    1.375       1.5     1.4375

    Recalculate  6 |    1.375     1.4375   1.40625


                      Formulas (R)

             A                  B                       C
      |---------|------------------------------|----------|-
    3 | START>   0
    4 | LEFT     RIGHT                            MID
    5 | 1        2
    6 | <A6>     @IF(B3=0,B5,@IF(A6=C6,B6,C6))    (A6+B6)/2

      A6: @IF(B3=0,A5,@IF((A6*A6-2)*(C6*C6-2)>0,C6,A6))
```

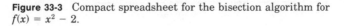

Figure 33-3   Compact spreadsheet for the bisection algorithm for $f(x) = x^2 - 2$.

33-4 EULER'S METHOD

This example is developed for

$$y' = x + y \qquad y(0) = 1$$

Euler's method for obtaining a numerical approximation to the solution of an IVP was presented in Demonstration 10. The spreadsheet in Figure 33-4 allows the number of iterations of the algorithm to be increased indefinitely. While the entry in cell C5 is 0, the initial values of x and y are copied into row 9 and the first 100 iterations are generated. When the value of C5 is set to 1 and with each subsequent recalculation, the values in row 109 are copied into row 9 and an additional 100 iterations are carried out. This scheme can be readily adapted to other iterative algorithms.

Exercises and Modifications

33-1. Modify the compact Fibonacci spreadsheet so that it contains a cell which calculates the quotient a_{n+1}/a_n, the values of which converge to the golden ratio.

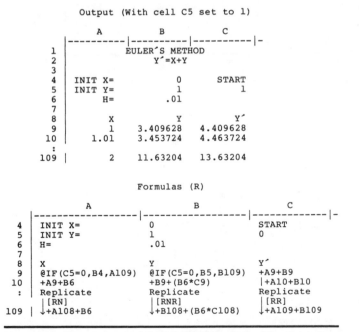

```
                 Output (With cell C5 set to 1)

                  A            B            C
          |----------|----------|----------|-
        1               EULER'S METHOD
        2                  Y'=X+Y
        3
        4    INIT X=          0        START
        5    INIT Y=          1            1
        6        H=         .01
        7
        8        X           Y           Y'
        9        1    3.409628     4.409628
       10     1.01    3.453724     4.463724
        :
      109 |      2    11.63204     13.63204


                     Formulas (R)

              A                    B                    C
       |-------------------|-------------------|-------------|-
     4  INIT X=            0                   START
     5  INIT Y=            1                   0
     6  H=                .01
     7
     8  X                  Y                   Y'
     9  @IF(C5=0,B4,A109)  @IF(C5=0,B5,B109)   +A9+B9
    10  +A9+B6             +B9+(B6*C9)         |+A10+B10
     :  Replicate          Replicate           Replicate
        |[RN]              |[RNR]               |[RR]
   109 |↓+A108+B6          ↓+B108+(B6*C108)    ↓+A109+B109
```

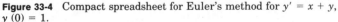

Figure 33-4 Compact spreadsheet for Euler's method for $y' = x + y$, $y(0) = 1$.

33-2. Modify the compact factorial spreadsheet to calculate terms of the sequence $1, 1 + 2, 1 + 2 + 3, 1 + 2 + 3 + 4, \ldots$.

33-3. Create a compact spreadsheet to compute x^n for $n = 1, 2, 3, \ldots$.

33-4. Create a compact spreadsheet for the fixed-point algorithm (Demonstration 4).

33-5. Modify the bisection spreadsheet to handle the case where one of the midpoints is itself a zero (see Exercise 3-1).

33-6. Use the technique employed in the compact Euler spreadsheet to modify the numerical-integration spreadsheet of Demonstration 8.

Matrix Powers

If A is a square matrix, powers of A are defined using matrix multiplication (see Demonstration 12) by

$$A^1 = A \qquad A^2 = A \cdot A \qquad A^3 = A \cdot A \cdot A \qquad \cdots$$

In general, $A^{n+1} = A \cdot A^n$. The spreadsheet in Figure 34-1 computes the powers $A^1, A^2, A^4, A^8, \ldots$ for a 2×2 matrix A. The extension to 3×3 and higher-dimension matrices is straightforward.

In moving from one power to the next the first row of the old power of A is used in computing the last row of the new power of A. Thus, at each stage, the current power of A must be saved while the new power is being computed. This is done in the spreadsheet by first copying the old power from rows 15 and 16 into rows 12 and 13 and then calculating the new power in rows 15 and 16.

Cell D7 is used to initialize the spreadsheet. After D7 has been set to a nonzero value and with each recalculation thereafter, the previously computed power is first copied and then used to compute the next power. By modifying the expressions in cells ‖B15 to C16‖ slightly, e.g., enter (B9*B12)+(C9*B13) into cell B15, all the powers A^n, $n = 1, 2, 3,$ 4, 5, . . . , will be generated. Cells D12 and D15 serve as counters.

In this example the entries in A are positive, and the sum of each column is 1. Matrices having this property arise in probability theory and physics as transition matrices of regular Markov processes [27, 40]. For large powers of such a matrix A the columns are eventually constant and identical (these columns are eigenvectors of A) and $A^{n+1} = A^n$ [36].

SPREADSHEET CONSTRUCTION

1. Enter the first row of the matrix A into cells B9 and C9. Enter $1-B9$ and $1-C9$ into cells B10 and C10 to ensure that the columns will add to 1. Alternatively, enter the second row of A into B10 and C10 directly.

2. Enter the indicated counter expressions into cells D12 and D15.

3. Enter a 0 into cell D7 to initialize the process.

4. The original matrix is copied into cells ‖B12 to C13‖ while D7 is 0; if D7 is set to a nonzero value, cells ‖B15 to C16‖ are copied into these cells (enter the formulas shown). Next, enter the indicated expressions into cells ‖B15 to C16‖ to form the square of the current matrix in cells ‖B12 to C13‖.

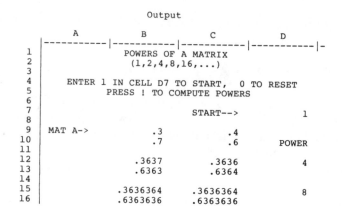

```
                             Output
                A           B           C           D
        |-----------|------------|------------|------------|-
     1                    POWERS OF A MATRIX
     2                     (1,2,4,8,16,...)
     3
     4          ENTER 1 IN CELL D7 TO START,   0 TO RESET
     5                  PRESS ! TO COMPUTE POWERS
     6
     7                               START-->            1
     8
     9   MAT A->              .3          .4
    10                        .7          .6          POWER
    11
    12                      .3637       .3636            4
    13                      .6363       .6364
    14
    15                    .3636364    .3636364           8
    16                    .6363636    .6363636
```

```
                             Formulas (R)
            A              B                    C                      D
        |----------|--------------------|----------------------|------------------|-
     7                           START-->                1
     8
     9   MAT A->    .3                   .4
    10              1-B9                 1-C9                   POWER
    11
    12              @IF(D7=0,B9,B15)     @IF(D7=0,C9,C15)       @IF(D7=0,1,D15)
    13              @IF(D7=0,B10,B16)    @IF(D7=0,C10,C16)
    14
    15              (B12*B12)+(C12*B13)  (B12*C12)+(C12*C13)    2*D12
    16              (B13*B12)+(C13*B13)  (B13*C12)+(C13*C13)
```

Figure 34-1 Matrix powers.

USER INTERACTION

Change the entries of the matrix. To retain columns adding to 1, change only cells B9 and C9. Change cells B10 and C10 to generate other 2 × 2 matrices.

Exercises and Modifications

34-1. Modify the product cells ‖B15 to C16‖ so that all the powers A^n of A, $n = 1, 2, 3, 4, \ldots$, will be generated as the spreadsheet is recalculated. Also modify the counter (D15).

34-2. Create spreadsheets to find powers of 3 × 3, 4 × 4, and 5 × 5 matrices.

34-3. Examine books on linear algebra, finite mathematics, or probability for discussions of Markov chains and transition matrices. Consider the following problem. Each year a percentage of voters switch their party registration. Suppose that each year switching is given by the following transition matrix:

	This year	
	Democrat	Republican
Next year		
Democrat	0.7	0.2
Republican	0.3	0.8

What percentage of the voters will be registered Democrats (Republicans) in the long run? The answer is that powers of the matrix will converge to a matrix in which each column contains the long-range probabilities. References 40 and 46 give examples from genetics, demographics, etc.

34-4. Create a compact spreadsheet which calculates $A^n\mathbf{v}$ for a 2 × 2 matrix A, a 2 × 1 vector $\mathbf{v}$, and $n = 1, 2, 3, \ldots$.

34-5. Modify the spreadsheet so that the rows, rather than the columns, of matrix A add to 1.

REFERENCES

Matrix powers: references 1, 10, 18, 36, and 40.

Markov chains and stochastic processes: references 10, 27, 36, 40, 46, and 64.

Systems of
Linear Equations
Elementary Matrices

The most widely used algorithm for solving a system of linear equations is *gaussian elimination,* or *gaussian pivoting.* This algorithm tends to be unwieldy to implement on a spreadsheet (see Demonstrations 30 and 31, where it is used). Nevertheless, gaussian elimination can be carried out through a series of multiplications by elementary matrices, operations easily implemented on a spreadsheet (see Demonstration 12).

Since a complete description of gaussian elimination is too long to give here, the algorithm will be illustrated by an example. The reader is referred to almost any book on linear algebra [1, 64] for a full discussion of the subject. The use of elementary matrices is examined in Ref. 35, pp. 66–69 and Ref. 64, pp. 55–58.

Example: $2x + 3y = 7$

$\quad\quad\quad\; 2x + \; y = 4$

Matrix form: $\begin{bmatrix} 2 & 3 & | & 7 \\ 2 & 1 & | & 4 \end{bmatrix}$

In the gaussian elimination that follows the use of equations is demonstrated on the left and that of elementary matrices on the right.

1. Multiply the first equation by ½

$$x + \tfrac{3}{2}y = \tfrac{7}{2}$$
$$2x + \quad y = 4$$

$$\begin{bmatrix} \tfrac{1}{2} & 0 \\ 0 & 1 \end{bmatrix} \begin{bmatrix} 2 & 3 & | & 7 \\ 2 & 1 & | & 4 \end{bmatrix} = \begin{bmatrix} 1 & \tfrac{3}{2} & | & \tfrac{7}{2} \\ 2 & 1 & | & 4 \end{bmatrix}$$

2. Add -2 times the first equation to the second equation

$$\begin{aligned} x + 3/2\,y &= 7/2 \\ -2y &= -3 \end{aligned} \qquad \begin{bmatrix} 1 & 0 \\ -2 & 1 \end{bmatrix}\begin{bmatrix} 1 & 3/2 & | & 7/2 \\ 2 & 1 & | & 4 \end{bmatrix} = \begin{bmatrix} 1 & 3/2 & | & 7/2 \\ 0 & -2 & | & -3 \end{bmatrix}$$

3. Multiply the second equation by $-1/2$:

$$\begin{aligned} x + 3/2\,y &= 7/2 \\ y &= 3/2 \end{aligned} \qquad \begin{bmatrix} 1 & 0 \\ 0 & -1/2 \end{bmatrix}\begin{bmatrix} 1 & 3/2 & | & 7/2 \\ 0 & -2 & | & -3 \end{bmatrix} = \begin{bmatrix} 1 & 3/2 & | & 7/2 \\ 0 & 1 & | & 3/2 \end{bmatrix}$$

4. Add $(-3/2)$ times the second equation to the first equation

$$\begin{aligned} x &= 5/4 \\ y &= 3/2 \end{aligned} \qquad \begin{bmatrix} 1 & -3/2 \\ 0 & 1 \end{bmatrix}\begin{bmatrix} 1 & 3/2 & | & 7/2 \\ 0 & 1 & | & 3/2 \end{bmatrix} = \begin{bmatrix} 1 & 0 & | & 5/4 \\ 0 & 1 & | & 3/2 \end{bmatrix}$$

The final system (or matrix) gives the answer, $x = 5/4$, $y = 3/2$.

The spreadsheet in Figures 35-1 and 35-2 carries out the matrix operations in rows 16 and 17. After setting cell A9 to 1, the user repeatedly manipulates the pivot matrix of cells ‖A16 to B17‖, alternatively creating elementary matrices and then restoring the identity matrix until the identity matrix is obtained in cells ‖C16 to D17‖. Either the value of a cell or the cell location can be used. Each time a new matrix is formed, a copy of cells ‖C21 to E22‖ is made in cells ‖C16 to E17‖ and the product of cells ‖C16 to E17‖ and the elementary matrix is computed in cells ‖C21 to E22‖. The final answer is shown in row 19.

```
                          Output

          A         B         C         D         E
      ---------|---------|---------|---------|---------|-
 1                    GAUSSIAN PIVOTING
 2
 3                      2X+3Y=7
 4                      2X+ Y=4
 5
 6    ENTER 1 TO START, 0 TO RESET. MANIPULATE PIVOT
 7    MATRIX TO OBTAIN IDENTITY MATRIX UNDER X, Y.
 8
 9        0     <-START        X         Y        CON
10
11                             2         3         7
12                             2         1         4
13
14    PIVOT MATRIX             X         Y        CON
15
16        1         0          2         3         7
17        0         1          2         1         4
18
19    ANSWER:   X=            NA        Y=         NA
20
21         CURRENT:            2         3         7
22                             2         1         4
```

Figure 35-1 Systems of linear equations: elementary matrices, output.

SPREADSHEET CONSTRUCTION

1. Enter the matrix of the equation into cells ‖C11 to E12‖ and the identity matrix into cells ‖A16 to B17‖.

2. Enter the indicated expressions into cells ‖C16 to E17‖ and ‖C21 to E22‖. The expressions in cells ‖C21 to E22‖ calculate the product of the pivot matrix and cells ‖C16 to E17‖. The expressions in cells ‖C16 to E17‖ copy the original matrix when A9 is 0; otherwise they copy the previous product from cells ‖C21 to E22‖.

3. The x, y coordinates of the answer are displayed in cells C19 and E19. The not-available symbol NA appears in cell C19 unless x has

Operation and Output

(1) Set A9 to 1:

	A	B	C	D	E
16	1	0	2	3	7
17	0	1	2	1	4

(2) Enter 1/2, then 1 into A16:

	A	B	C	D	E
16	1	0	1	1.5	3.5
17	0	1	2	1	4

(3) Enter -2, then 0 into A17:

	A	B	C	D	E
16	1	0	1	1.5	3.5
17	0	1	0	-2	-3

(4) Enter 1/-2, then 1 into B17:

	A	B	C	D	E
16	1	0	1	1.5	3.5
17	0	1	0	1	1.5

(5) Enter -1.5, then 0 into B16:

	A	B	C	D	E
16	1	0	1	0	1.25
17	0	1	0	1	1.5

Solution:

$x = 1.25$

$y = 1.5$

Formulas (R)

	A	B	C	D	E
9	0	<ST	X	Y	CON
10					
11			2	3	7
12			2	1	4
13					
14	PIV	MAT	X	Y	CON
15					
16	1	0	@IF(A9=0,C11,C21)	@IF(A9=0,D11,D21)	@IF(A9=0,E11,E21)
17	0	1	@IF(A9=0,C12,C22)	@IF(A9=0,D12,D22)	@IF(A9=0,E12,E22)
18					
19	ANS	X=	@IF(@AND(C16=1, D16=0),E16,@NA)	Y=	@IF(@AND(C17=0, D17=1),E17,@NA)
20					
21		CUR	(A16*C16)+(B16*C17) (A17*C16)+(B17*C17)	(A16*D16)+(B16*D17) (A17*D16)+(B17*D17)	(A16*E16)+(B16*E17) (A17*E16)+(B17*E17)
22					

Figure 35-2 Systems of linear equations; elementary matrices, operation and output, and formulas.

been determined; that is, C16 = 1 and D16 = 0, in which case x = E16. Enter

$$@IF(@AND(C16=1,D16=0),E16,@NA)$$

into cell C19. The entry in cell E19 is similar.

USER INTERACTION

1. Set A9 to 0 to reinitialize the process; set A9 to 1 to begin.
2. Change the coefficients of the equations in cells ‖C11 to E12‖.
3. Manipulate the pivot matrix in cells ‖A16 to B17‖ to solve the system of equations. There are many valid ways of proceeding. Cell locations may be used instead of cell values; in steps 2 to 5 above, use 1/C16, −C17, 1/D17, and −D16.

Exercises and Modifications

35-1. Because of computer roundoff, cells ‖C16 to D17‖ may differ slightly from the identity matrix after the pivoting process. In this case answers will fail to appear in cells C19 and E19. Modify the spreadsheet to handle this situation.

35-2. Modify the coefficients in the spreadsheet to solve the system $2x - 9y = 8, 5x + 3y = 7$.

35-3. Solve the system $3x - 7y = 9, -6x + 14y = -18$ using the spreadsheet. It does not have a unique solution, but the solution can be read off the final matrix.

35-4. Use the spreadsheet to show that the system $3x + 2y = 8, 6x + 4y = 3$ has no solution.

35-5. Create a spreadsheet to use appropriate elementary matrices to solve n equations in m unknowns for various n and m.

35-6. Using columns E and F, modify the spreadsheet algorithm to find the inverse of the matrix A. Replace the single column vector $[7 \quad 4]^T$ by the two-column identity matrix

$$\begin{bmatrix} 1 & 0 \\ 0 & 1 \end{bmatrix}$$

and repeat the steps.

REFERENCES

Gaussian elimination: references 1, 11, 23, 35, 36, 48, 53, 59, and 64.

Elementary matrices: references 35, 48, and 64.

Boundary-Value Problems

Many physical problems can be modeled using partial differential equations. For example, the steady-state heat distribution in a thin rectangular plate, $1 \leqslant x \leqslant 12$, $4 \leqslant y \leqslant 20$, which is held at $0°C$ on the boundaries $y = 4$ and $y = 20$ while the temperature along the other two boundaries is held at $f(y) = 80 - 10|y - 12|$ is given by Laplace's equation [11, 23]

$$u_{xx}(x, y) + u_{yy}(x, y) = 0$$

for

$$(x, y) \text{ in } R = \{(x, y) \mid 1 < x < 12, 4 < y < 20\}$$

with boundary conditions

$$u(x, 4) = u(x, 20) = 0 \qquad 1 \leqslant x \leqslant 12$$
$$u(1, y) = u(12, y) = f(y) \qquad 4 \leqslant y \leqslant 20$$

An intuitive and easily described iterative technique uses selected mesh points in the plate to approximate convergence to the steady-state distribution. In this example the mesh points are those with integer coordinates

$$\{(i, j) \mid i = 1, 2, \ldots, 12; j = 4, 5, \ldots, 20\}$$

Start with an initial temperature distribution of $0°C$ at all interior mesh points and at the given fixed temperatures at mesh points on the boundary. Then, if $u^{(n)}(i, j)$ represents the nth iterative temperature estimate at (i, j), the Gauss-Seidel algorithm [30, p. 279] gives the $(n + 1)$th temperature estimate at an interior point (i, j)

$$u^{(n+1)}(i, j) =$$

$$\frac{u^{(n+1)}(i - 1, j) + u^{(n+1)}(i, j - 1) + u^{(n)}(i, j + 1) + u^{(n)}(i + 1, j)}{4}$$

Thus, the $(n + 1)$th temperature estimate at (i, j) is simply the average of the most recent approximations of the temperatures of the four adjacent points.

This algorithm can be implemented in a straightforward manner on a spreadsheet (Figure 36-1), providing an easily visualized model of the heat flow and the model's convergence to steady state. Cell A2 is used to initialize the spreadsheet. To begin the process, set A2 to a nonzero value. To carry out the iterations, press the recalculate key

Output (Early in progress toward steady-state)

	A	B	C	D	E	F	G	H	I	J	K	L
1						HEAT	-	LA PLACE				
2	1	<--START								N=	11	
3												
4	0	0	0	0	0	0	0	0	0	0	0	0
5	10	7	5	3	2	2	1	2	3	5	7	10
6	20	15	10	7	5	3	3	4	7	10	15	20
7	30	22	16	11	7	5	5	6	10	16	23	30
8	40	30	21	14	10	7	6	9	14	21	30	40
9	50	37	26	18	12	9	8	11	17	26	38	50
10	60	44	31	21	14	10	10	13	20	31	45	60
11	70	50	35	23	16	11	11	15	23	35	51	70
12	80	54	37	24	16	12	12	15	24	37	54	80
13	70	51	35	24	16	12	12	15	23	35	51	70
14	60	45	32	22	15	11	11	15	22	32	45	60
15	50	38	28	19	13	10	10	13	19	28	38	50
16	40	31	23	16	11	9	9	11	16	23	31	40
17	30	23	17	12	9	7	7	9	12	17	24	30
18	20	16	12	8	6	5	5	6	8	12	16	20
19	10	8	6	4	3	3	3	3	4	6	8	10
20	0	0	0	0	0	0	0	0	0	0	0	0

Formulas (R)

	A	B	...	K	L
2	0	<--		@IF(A2=0,0,1+K2)	
3					
4	0	0	..	0	0
5	10	@IF(A2=0,0,(B4+A5+B6+C5)/4)	..	@IF(A2=0,0,(K4+J5+K6+L5)/4)	10
6	20	@IF(A2=0,0,(B5+A6+B7+C6)/4)	..	@IF(A2=0,0,(K5+J6+K7+L6)/4)	20
:					
19	10	@IF(A2=0,0, (B18+A19+B20+C19)/4)	..	@IF(A2=0,0, (K18+J19+K20+L19)/4)	10
20	0	0	..	0	0

Replicate: Rows,Columns [NRRRR]

Figure 36-1 Boundary-value problems.

repeatedly (this can be done without waiting for the screen to show the complete recalculation). Cell K2 is used as a counter. Integer format is used to improve screen display.

SPREADSHEET CONSTRUCTION

1. Enter the initial distribution into rows 4 and 20 and columns A and L.

2. Cell K2 is a counter. Enter @IF(A2=0,0,1+K2).

3. If cell A2 is set to zero, the value of cell B5 and each interior cell is 0. Otherwise each cell is set to the average of the values of the four adjacent cells. Enter

$$@IF(A2=0,0,(B4+A5+B6+C5)/4)$$

into cell B5.

4. To enter the average of adjacent cells into all interior cells, replicate the expression in B5 into cells C5 to K5; then replicate row 5 (columns B to K) into rows 6 to 19, with all locations relative.

USER INTERACTION

Change boundary conditions (rows 4 and 20; columns A and L).

Exercises and Modifications

36-1. Use the spreadsheet to find the steady-state solution of the heat problem if the upper boundary is held at 0°C, the bottom boundary at 80°C, and the side boundaries at temperatures which vary linearly from top to bottom.

36-2. Convergence toward steady state can be increased by using the technique of overrelaxation [30, p. 279]. This technique can be viewed as follows. Let

$$B = \frac{u^{(n+1)}(i-1, j) + u^{(n+1)}(i, j-1) + u^{(n)}(i, j+1) + u^{(n)}(i+1, j)}{4}$$

In the Gauss-Seidel algorithm new values of $u^{(n+1)}$ are computed by

$$u^{(n+1)}(i, j) = u^{(n)}(i, j) + [B - u^{(n)}(i, j)]$$

that is, in going from step n to step $n + 1$ the temperature in cell (i, j) is increased by $B - u^{(n)}(i, j)$. The overrelaxation technique multiplies this increase by a factor of $t > 1$ to obtain

$$u^{(n+1)}(i, j) = u^{(n)}(i, j) + t[B - u^{(n)}(i, j)]$$
$$= (1 - t)u^{(n)}(i, j) + tB$$

To implement this in the spreadsheet simply enter the value for t into cell F2, modify the expression in cell B5 to

@IF(A2=0,0,(1−F2)*B5+(F2*(B4+A5+B6+C5)/4))

and replicate this throughout the spreadsheet (using [NNRNRRRR]) as in the original construction. If t is too large, the algorithm becomes unstable. The value $t = 1.6$ works well for this example. Create a spreadsheet to solve the heat-flow problem using the Gauss-Seidel algorithm with overrelaxation.

36-3. Create a spreadsheet to model the one-dimensional heat-flow problem in a uniform thin rod. Suppose that the rod is initially at 0°C and the left end is held at 30°C and the right end at 80°C. Create a model to find the steady-state temperatures. At each stage the temperature of a point is the average of the temperatures of the two adjacent points on either side.

36-4. Repeat Exercise 36-3 using overrelaxation.

36-5. Examine references for iterative models of similar boundary-value problems and use a spreadsheet to implement them.

REFERENCES

Heat-equation and boundary-value problems: references 11, 23, and 30.

Appendix

Some Multiplan Adaptations

Multiplan is another popular spreadsheet program. The demonstrations in this book can be readily translated from VisiCalc into Multiplan with the aid of a Multiplan user's manual. This appendix contains some additional observations that will simplify that process.

In Multiplan, both rows and columns are identified by positive integers. Formulas may contain both absolute and relative references to cell locations. For example, each of the formulas 1+R5C3 and 1+R[+2]C[−1] will generate the same output when entered into cell R3C4 (row 3, column 4). The Multiplan COPY command replicates formulas exactly as they are written. Thus, a formula to be copied must contain relative cell references for relative (R) replication and absolute cell references for constant (N) replication. For example, in Demonstration 10 the entry in cell R10C2 would be +R[−1]C+(R6C2*R[−1]C[+1]).

The VisiCalc @CHOOSE function can be translated by the Multiplan INDEX function. However, unlike the @CHOOSE function which can select a value from a list of formulas, the INDEX function can only select a value from a range of cells. Thus, each formula which appears in a @CHOOSE function must be placed in a separate cell for use with INDEX. For example, if Multiplan cells R1C1, R1C2, and R1C3 contain the same values as VisiCalc cells A1, B1, and C1, then @CHOOSE(A1,B1+C1,B1*C1,1+B1) can be translated as INDEX(R1C5:R1C7,R1C1), where cell R1C5 contains +R1C2+R1C3, cell R1C6 contains +R1C2*R1C3, and cell R1C7 contains 1+R1C2. This technique must be used repeatedly with Demonstrations 30 and 31.

Multiplan uses a sophisticated method for recalculating the spreadsheet which eliminates the need to specify the order of calculation. However, Multiplan's default setting does not allow for circular references, such as are used in Demonstrations 33 to 36. To implement these demonstrations in Multiplan, adopt the following scheme:

1. Enter the Boolean expression ITERCNT( )>=0 into cell R1C1.

2. Using the OPTIONS command, set the iteration option to "yes" and the test cell to R1C1.

3. Translate each VisiCalc formula that has the form

    $$@IF(A3=0,f1,f2),$$

    where A3 is an initialization cell, into the Multiplan formula

    $$IF(R3C1=0,f1,IF(ISNA(R1C1),f2,RC)).$$

    For example, in Figure 33-1 the entry in cell R5C1 would be IF(R3C1=0,0,IF(ISNA(R1C1),1+R5C1,RC)). There are two exceptions: in Demonstration 35 replace each ISNA(R1C1) by NOT(ISNA(R1C1)); throughout Demonstration 34 use R18C1 in place of R1C1 unless constants (rather than formulas) are entered in the second row (row 10) of the original matrix.

4. Carry out iterations using the ! command.

References

A. General

1. Agnew, Jeanne, and Robert C. Knapp: *Linear Algebra with Applications,* 2d ed., Brooks/Cole, Monterey, Calif., 1983.

2. Anton, Howard: *Calculus with Analytic Geometry,* Wiley, New York, 1980.

3. Arganbright, Deane E.: Mathematical Applications of an Electronic Spreadsheet, *1984 Yearbook of the National Council of Teachers of Mathematics,* Reston, Va., 1984, pp. 184–193.

4. Arganbright, Deane E.: The Electronic Spreadsheet and Mathematical Algorithms, *The College Mathematics Journal,* March 1984, pp. 148–157.

5. Atkinson, Kendall E.: *An Introduction to Numerical Analysis,* Wiley, New York, 1978.

6. Beck, Anatole, Michael N. Bleicher, and Donald W. Crowe: *Excursions into Mathematics,* Worth, New York, 1969.

7. Beiler, Albert H.: *Recreations in the Theory of Numbers,* 2d ed., Dover, New York, 1966.

8. Berman, Gerald, and K. D. Fryer: *Introduction to Combinatorics,* Academic, New York, 1972.

9. Billstein, Rick, Shlomo Libeskind, and Johnny W. Lott: *Mathematics for Elementary School Teachers,* Benjamin/Cummings, Menlo Park, Calif., 1981.

10. Brown, Robert F., and Brenda W. Brown: *Applied Finite Mathematics,* Wadsworth, Belmont, Calif., 1977.

11. Burden, Richard L., J. Douglas Faires, and Albert C. Reynolds: *Numerical Analysis,* 2d ed., Prindle, Weber and Schmidt, Boston, 1981.

12. Burton, David M.: *Elementary Number Theory,* Allyn and Bacon, Boston, 1980.

13. Castlewitz, David M., and Lawrence J. Chisausky: *VisiCalc Home and Office Companion,* Osborne/McGraw-Hill, Berkeley, Calif., 1982.

14. Chvatal, Vasek: *Linear Programming,* Freeman, New York, 1983.

15. Cobb, Douglas Ford, and Gene Berg Cobb: *Supercalc Models for Business,* Que, Indianapolis, 1983.

16. Cohen, Daniel I. A.: *Basic Techniques of Combinatorial Theory,* Wiley, New York, 1978.

17. Dobbs, David, and Robert Hanks: *A Modern Course in the Theory of Equations,* Polygonal, Passaic, N.J., 1980.

18. Dorn, William S., and Daniel D. McCracken: *Introductory Finite Mathematics with Computing,* Wiley, New York, 1976.

19. Drooyan, Irving, and Bill Rosen: *Intermediate Algebra: A Guided Worktext,* Wadsworth, Belmont, Calif., 1983.

20. Elich, Joseph, and Carletta J. Elich: *Precalculus with Calculator Applications,* Addison-Wesley, Reading, Mass., 1982.

21. Flegg, Graham: *Numbers,* Schocken, New York, 1983.

22. Fossum, Timothy V., and Ronald W. Gatterdam: *Calculus and the Computer,* Scott, Foresman, Glenview, Ill., 1980.

22a. Geist, Robert: How to Live to be 100, *The College Mathematics Journal,* June 1984, pp. 256–263.

23. Gerald, Curtis F.: *Applied Numerical Analysis,* 2d ed., Addison-Wesley, Reading, Mass., 1978.

24. Gere, James M., and William Weaver, Jr.: *Matrix Algebra for Engineers,* 2d ed., Brooks/Cole, Monterey, Calif., 1983.

25. Gibney, Frank Jr.: The Tail That Wags the Dog, *Newsweek,* Feb. 22, 1982, p. 55.

26. Goldstein, Herbert: *Classical Mechanics,* 2d ed., Addison-Wesley, Reading, Mass., 1980.

27. Goldstein, Larry J., and David I. Schneider: *Finite Mathematics and Its Applications,* Prentice-Hall, Englewood Cliffs, N.J., 1980.

28. Henrici, Peter: *Elements of Numerical Analysis,* Wiley, New York, 1964.

29. Hoggatt, Verner E. Jr.: *Fibonacci and Lucas Numbers,* Houghton Mifflin, Boston, 1969.

30. Hornbeck, Robert W.: *Numerical Methods,* Prentice-Hall/Quantum, Englewood Cliffs, N.J., 1975.

31. Huntley, H. E.: *The Divine Proportion,* Dover, New York, 1970.

32. Huntsberger, David V., and Patrick Billingsley: *Elements of Statistical Inference,* 5th ed., Allyn and Bacon, Boston, 1981.

33. Jacobs, Harold R.: *Mathematics: A Human Endeavor,* 2d ed., Freeman, San Francisco, 1982.

34. Keedy, Mervin L., and Marvin L. Bittinger: *Fundamental Algebra and Trigonometry,* 2d ed., Addison-Wesley, Reading, Mass., 1981.

35. Kenschaft, Patricia Clark: *Linear Algebra: A Practical Approach,* Worth, New York, 1978.

36. Kolman, Bernard: *Introductory Linear Algebra with Applications,* 2d ed., Macmillan, New York, 1980.

37. Kraitchik, Maurice: *Mathematical Recreations,* 2d ed., Dover, New York, 1953.

38. Liu, C. L.: *Introduction to Combinatorial Mathematics,* McGraw-Hill, New York, 1968.

39. Long, Calvin T.: *Elementary Introduction to Number Theory,* 2d ed., Heath, Lexington, Mass., 1972.

40. Maki, Daniel P., and Maynard Thompson: *Finite Mathematics,* 2d ed., McGraw-Hill, New York, 1983.

41. Mendenhall, William: *Introduction to Probability and Statistics,* 5th ed., Duxbury, North Scituate, Mass., 1979.

42. Miller, Charles D., and Vern E. Heeren: *Mathematical Ideas,* 4th ed., Scott, Foresman, Glenview, Ill., 1983.

43. Mizrahi, Abe, and Michael Sullivan: *Calculus and Analytic Geometry,* Wadsworth, Belmont, Calif., 1982.

44. Olds, C. D.: *Continued Fractions,* Mathematical Association of America, Washington, 1963.

45. Ore, Øystein: *Number Theory and Its History,* McGraw-Hill, New York, 1948.

46. Rorres, Chris, and Howard Anton: *Applications of Linear Algebra,* Wiley, New York, 1977.

47. Ross, Kenneth A.: *Elementary Analysis: The Theory of Calculus,* Springer-Verlag, New York, 1980.

48. Shields, Paul C.: *Elementary Linear Algebra,* 3d ed., Worth, New York, 1980.

49. Singleton, Robert R., and William F. Tyndall: *Games and Programs: Mathematics for Modeling,* Freeman, San Francisco, 1974.

50. Stancl, Donald L., and Mildred L. Stancl: *Applications of College Mathematics,* Heath, Lexington, Mass., 1983.

51. Stark, Harold M.: *An Introduction to Number Theory,* The MIT Press, Cambridge, Mass., 1979.

52. Stein, Robert G.: *Mathematics: An Exploratory Approach,* McGraw-Hill, New York, 1975.

53. Strang, Gilbert: *Linear Algebra and Its Applications,* 2d ed., Academic, New York, 1980.

54. Strum, Jay E.: *Introduction to Linear Programming,* Holden-Day, San Francisco, 1972.

55. Swokowski, Earl W.: *Calculus with Analytic Geometry,* Prindle, Weber and Schmidt, Boston, 1979.

56. Trost, Stanley R.: *Doing Business with SuperCalc,* Sybex, Berkeley, Calif., 1983.

57. Trost, Stanley R.: *Doing Business with VisiCalc,* Sybex, Berkeley, Calif., 1982.

58. Tucker, Alan: *Applied Combinatorics,* Wiley, New York, 1980.

59. Vandergraft, James S.: *Introduction to Numerical Computations,* 2d ed., Academic, New York, 1983.

60. Varga, Richard S.: *Matrix Iterative Analysis,* Prentice-Hall, Englewood Cliffs, N.J., 1962.

61. Vilenkin, N. Y.: *Methods of Successive Approximations,* Mir, Moscow, 1979.

62. Walpole, Ronald E.: *Introduction to Statistics,* 3d ed., Macmillan, New York, 1982.

63. Wheeler, Ruric E., and W. D. Peeples, Jr.: *Modern Mathematics with Applications to Business and the Social Sciences,* 3d ed., Brooks/Cole, Monterey, Calif., 1980.

64. Yaqub, Adil, and Hal G. Moore: *Elementary Linear Algebra with Applications,* Addison-Wesley, Reading, Mass., 1980.

65. Zill, Dennis G.: *A First Course in Differential Equations with Applications,* Prindle, Weber and Schmidt, Boston, 1979.

B. Electronic Spreadsheet Operation

66. Anborlian, Harry: *An Introduction to VisiCalc Matrixing for Apple and IBM,* McGraw-Hill, New York, 1982.

67. Beil, Donald H.: *SuperCalc! The Book,* Reston, Reston, Va., 1983.

68. Beil, Donald H.: *The VisiCalc Book* (Atari, Apple, IBM editions), Reston, Reston, Va., 1982–1983.

69. Castlewitz, David M.: *The VisiCalc Program Made Easy,* Osborne/McGraw-Hill, Berkeley, Calif., 1983.

70. Desautels, Edouard J.: *VisiCalc for the IBM Personal Computer,* William C. Brown, Dubuque, Iowa, 1982.

71. Fylstra, D., and B. Kling: *VisiCalc User's Guide for the Apple II Plus,* Personal Software, Sunnyvale, Calif., 1981.

72. Herbert, Douglas: *Mastering VisiCalc,* Sybex, Berkeley, Calif., 1983.

73. LeBlond, Geoffrey T., and Douglas Ford Cobb: *Using 1-2-3,* Que, Indianapolis, 1983.

74. Schware, Robert, and Alice Trembour: *All about 1-2-3,* Dilithium, Beaverton, Ore., 1983.

75. Williams, Robert E.: *The Power of 1-2-3 for the IBM PC,* Management Information Source, Portland, Ore., 1982.

76. Williams, Robert E., and Bruce J. Taylor: *The Power of VisiCalc,* 2d ed., Management Information Source, Portland, Ore., 1981.

Index